To Jan— Best Wishes
[illegible]

MW01707001

The Pause in my Life: The Story of Andy

By Joan Bodefeld

Joan Bodefeld

JUPITER4PRESS

Published by Jupiter4Press in cooperation and by arrangement with the author

Cover designed by Michael Blackett and Steve Ainley

Jupiter4Press
P.O. Box 334
Schererville, IN 46375

The author is grateful for the assistance of James Bodefeld in compiling information, securing the photos, and assisting in obtaining permission to use document inserts in order to complete an accurate account of the life or part thereof of Nelson J. Anderson, Jr.

Acknowledgments

I wish to acknowledge and express my appreciation to my family and friends for their encouragement and support. I hope you enjoy reading my book as much as I enjoyed writing it.

I especially thank my daughter, Mary Davis, my grandson, Michael Davis, my son, Steve Ainley, his wife Angie, my son, Dave Ainley and his wife Meg, for their technical skills. I thank my dear husband, Jim, for his loving patience and guidance. I thank my proof reader/ golfing partner/ good friend, Margaret Quinn, for her endurance, my neighbors, Dick Downs, also a barber, and his wife Judy, Karen Nowatski, Mary and Ted Tanis, and Joan Krager for their enthusiasm in my endeavor. I thank Diane Slavik, the receptionist for my dentist, Dr Ancich. She gave me a small book and a large boost to get me going. I thank Jim's sister, Carol Seering, for her continued good wishes and my Scherwood Ladies Wednesday Morning Golf League gals for our laughter and good times, on and off the course. I am grateful to my publisher, Michael Blackett and his wife Mary, for their expertise and to VAS for the opportunity. I am blessed! Lastly, I thank Nelson J. Anderson, Jr. and all his wonderful friends and family.

Dedicated to all who volunteer

Your kindness and energy are always appreciated and will not be unrewarded.

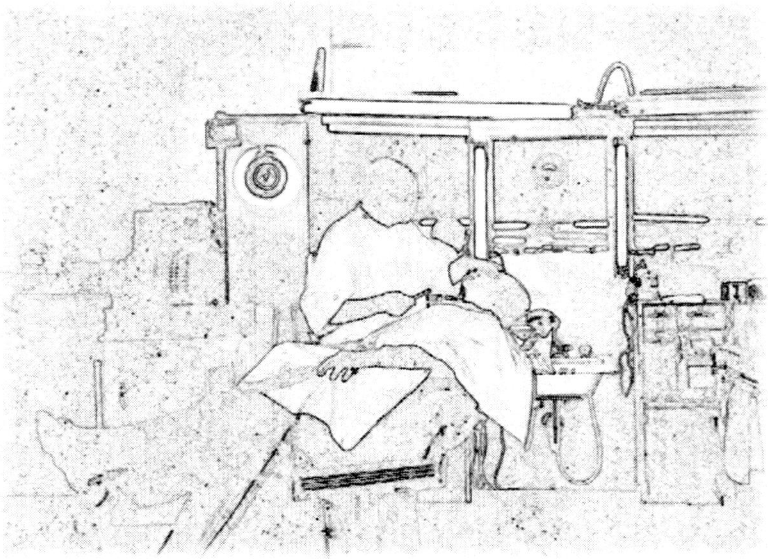

The Pause in my Life
The Story of Andy

By Joan Bodefeld

VAS - Volunteer Advocates for Seniors

About the program-taken from the website of Saint Margaret Mercy Health Care Center

www.volunteeradvocatesforseniors.org

Volunteer Advocates for Seniors Program (VAS) began in 2001 in partnership with the Lake Superior Court in an effort to address the health care and social service needs of the ever-increasing population of unbefriended elderly patients being served by the Saint Margaret Mercy Hospitals. Since then the SMM Hospital has worked with the Lake Superior Court, the local legal community and the major health care and social service providers in the region to establish the program. The VAS Program serves clients in the

SMM Hospitals in Hammond and Dyer, Indiana, and the Saint Anthony Hospital in Crown Point, Indiana. The program recently partnered with other local hospitals and nursing facilities to better serve the community.

The at-risk seniors served by the VAS Program are incapable of representing or protecting their own "best interests" and are without suitable family or guardian involvement to help them make decisions. Volunteers are required to complete a 40 hour course plus 12 hours continuing education annually. The role of the volunteer guardian is to assist the Court by investigating and assessing the at-risk person's life situation, facilitating health care and social services needed by the individual, and planning for the appropriate residential placement to best serve his or her needs.

Lake County Sheriff's Office
Incident Report
Lake County Sheriff's Department
Investigation Narrative

Reporting Officer:

On 10-31-2005 at 7:10A.M. Ofc. Breitweiser was dispatched to 15330 W. 101st in reference to an older black male found sleeping on the front lawn of the above address. The man was identified by Illinois driver's license as Nelson J. Anderson of Chicago, Illinois. Nelson advised he had taken the bus out to Gas City last night to eat because he liked the management. Once he left sometime later he advised he became disoriented, tried walking to the bus stop but didn't know where it was. Nelson advised the next thing he remembered was waking up this morning in the front yard of the above address. Nelson was transported by St. John EMS 2107 to St. Margaret's Hospital in Dyer because his body temperature was 95.5. Nelson was unable to advise of any relative's phone number who we could contact. This officer did find a phone number on a business card in Nelson's wallet of William Blair, President of Happy Action Seniors Club in Chicago. This officer spoke to William who advised Nelson was a member of the club and also his barber. William could not advise of any family members of Nelson's that he knew of but did agree that he would be en-route to pick Nelson up and take him home. This officer left William's phone number with the ER and advised them to call him when he could be released.

'Document Supplied by Lake County Sheriff's Office'

-1-

Daughter: "Mom, what's the point of the story? Why are you writing it? What's the point? Who's going to read it?"

Mom: "Point? There is no point. Why does there have to be a point? Can't it just be a little story about a little man who made a big impression on all the people he came in contact with? When through one man, a little more love and goodness, a little more light and truth come into the world, then that man's life has had meaning and I am going to write about it."

Daughter: "Mom, maybe that's the point."

-2-

My daily prayer calendar reads: It is good for me, Lord, to think about the wonderful things you have done. May my life overflow with gratitude today. Amen. Nov. 4th, 2005…He knew…!

Early that morning as I was baking cookies to take to work the next day, I received a phone call from Vanessa Nathan, Coordinator of the VAS Program, telling me she had a 79 year old gentleman who needed a guardian. (Patients are recommended for the program by the hospital social service department. The hospital then files a petition with the Lake Superior Court for a 60 day limited guardianship of the patient.) I distinctly remember thinking, “Oh, I have to work the next three days.” So I told her, “I’m not sure because I have to work over the weekend.

My weekend... I loved my weekend. I was the Charge Nurse in the Psychiatric Unit at St. Margaret Mercy Health Care Center with an incredible staff, Nurses Laura Gasper, Judith Beezley, and Susan Gerba; and, Behavioral Advisors, Jennifer Martin and Bob Tomaszewski. We worked together many years as a strong team. Saturday was always chocolate day and Sunday was pineapple. We looked forward to that.

Vanessa said that was perfect because he was already a patient at the South Campus so I could see him there. (The South Campus being St. Margaret Mercy Hospital, Dyer, Indiana.) She continued to tell me he was an Illinois resident without a known family and would need some medical procedures.

He had been brought in through the Emergency Room on Halloween morning by the paramedics after being found lying on the front lawn of a home in rural Dyer, Indiana. He said he "took a bus". He had been hospitalized in the ICU due to the severity of his condition. The court papers were filed and we (Jim, my husband, and I) were to be his guardians. The necessary papers would be in my mailbox when I returned to work the next morning. Okay, now I was getting excited. His name was Nelson J. Anderson.

It was exciting to be assigned a new case but there was also a lot of anxiety. As a Limited Guardian, you accept the responsibility of a person's care just as you would do with a family member and apparently Nelson had no one. Jim and I, as Limited Guardians, would represent and protect his interests and literally become his family. Kind of scary but we also knew from past experiences that we were capable of giving this gentleman the best of care and that we had the backing and the continued support of the VAS Program.

Vanessa Nathan is the Coordinator of the Program. Vanessa is a very charismatic person, devoted to the care and best interest of the incapacitated seniors. She gives strength to the Program through her exceptional knowledge and organizational skills.

The following day all the pertinent information was in my mailbox. I read it over on my lunch break. Meanwhile, I received a call from the hospital's Utilization Nurse, Barb Stark, saying that Nelson had a visitor. William Blair was asking for Nelson's keys to the barber shop. He told her the mail was piling up in between the storm doors. Actually, when a patient enters the hospital, any personal belongings are put in the hospital safe. In this case his keys and wallet were confined. I explained to Barb that this was not a good time but that if he left his name and number on Nelson's chart, I would get back to him. She agreed. Barb also mentioned that Mr. Blair said Nelson had a sister in Grand Rapids, Michigan by the name of Ruth. Okay, I would follow up after work.

At the end of my shift, I went to the medical floor. Jim met me on the Unit. Nelson had been transferred out of ICU. We first reviewed the chart. The contacts on the chart were William Blair, friend; and, Sgt. Tyrone Jordan of the Chicago Police Department. Nelson's date of birth was 07/18/26. His current address was given, we presumed, by Nelson, as 5702 S. Michigan Ave., Chicago, IL. The history and physical mentioned diabetes, heart failure, coronary plasty with stent, probable pneumonia, and NQWMI which stands for non q wave heart attack. Also mentioned is the failure of the patient to perform the MMSE. This is the Mini Mental State Examination which consists of 11 questions to assess the mental status in the areas of cognitive function, orientation, memory, attention and calculation, recall and language. This failure meant Nelson was incapacitated and needed an advocate for his rights. As guardians, we were to facilitate and authorize health care, social welfare and residential placement services as needed. We also would investigate and gather information regarding Nelson's health, welfare and financial circumstances as directed by the Court. As advocate, we are considered an Officer of the Court for this purpose and are supervised by the VAS Program. Mike Wertz from social services was to be his case manager while hospitalized. Cardiac rehab and occupational therapy (OT) and physical therapy (PT) were ordered by the physician. We were now ready to meet with Nelson.

Jim and I knocked on the door and entered Nelson's room. He was lying in bed with his eyes closed but quickly opened them and smiled at us saying, "I'm so glad to see you again." Jim shook his hand and I the same, except he held on to my hand and squeezed my fingers. That was the beginning of a very exceptional relationship. Nelson sat up a little straighter in bed while we tried to talk with him about himself. Yes, he was confused, but pleasantly. He was oriented to his person, knew his name, but not the time or place. We asked him about "taking a bus". He smiled, still holding my hand, and I was in love. He said, "I liked the food and the management." Then he stated, "I got a headache and laid down." He said it just like…no big deal. Nelson kept repeating, "I need my keys. I need my keys." Then he mentioned Missouri a few times and said he drove a Saab car. He did tell us he was a barber but not able to tell us where he lived. He said, "Well….you know, here and there." My first impression was, "What a sweetie, the VAS Program works well." After saying goodbye and telling Nelson that we would see him again soon, Jim and I proceeded with our credentials to the hospital security office to take a look at Nelson's safe packet.

At this point in the discovery, I always had the feeling of being nosy and invading a person's privacy, but kind of exciting too. There were two safe packet bags, one containing numerous charge cards in his wallet, seventeen in all, some current, some expired, five bank cards, all current, a card with the name and address of William Blair, Medicare and Civil Service Retirement System cards, Veteran Benefit card and a large amount of cash. There were also clues to the possibility of three vehicles, a 1982 Toyota, a 1977 Volkswagen bus and a 1969 Oldsmobile sedan. We wondered which car he drove to Indiana. That's where we would need to do some investigating and Jim was very good in that department. The second bag contained Nelson's glasses, some jewelry, his driver's license and "THE KEYS", a lot of keys! His driver's license read 650 E. 79th St., Chicago, IL born 7/18/1926, 5'5", 140 lbs., and brown eyes. I guessed no hair color because he was pretty much bald. But the address of 650 E. 79th St. was the shocker. My old neighborhood…I was born and raised there…81st and St. Lawrence Ave. My father had a pharmacy at 752 E. 79th St., Reel's Prescriptions. This was going to be a "reel" challenge. We returned the packets to security and would pick them up again when we were able to transport them to the St. Margaret Mercy North Campus VAS safe. I was still in awe that I could return to my old neighborhood. I couldn't wait to talk to Nelson about this, and then well, maybe not. We'll see.

-3-

The following day after work I again reviewed Nelson's chart and pulled up some reports on the computer. Mind you, my nursing career spans over 40 years…we just took a piece of paper called a nurse's note and a pen and wrote…but that's a different story.

Nelson has nasal oxygen, intravenous fluids and a foley catheter. His physicians, Drs. Michelle Osborn and Mohan Tadikond, agreed Nelson's mental and physical condition likely had been this way for many months with total dementia at this time. They say he is alert and cooperative but unable to sustain a meaningful conversation. The psychiatrist, Dr. Sandhu, also agreed and recommended legal guardianship along with medications, finances and safety monitoring.

I peeked in on Nelson. He was asleep and appeared to be resting comfortably.

What must he be thinking? He looked so small and lonely lying in the bed. What a job we had ahead of us. I looked forward to getting to know him.

When I returned home, I phoned and left a message for William Blair telling him that Jim and I were appointed guardians for his friend Nelson and we would greatly appreciate any information he was able to provide regarding any family members. He returned my call and spoke to Jim at length.

The information was that Nelson had a nephew, that Nelson owned two barber shops in Chicago, one he rented out, the Hair Affair on 95th St., and the other on 79th St. (both in Chicago) called Prince's Barber Shop. He operated this shop on a daily basis cutting hair by appointment only. Mr. Blair also thought there was a sister named Ruth who lived in Grand Rapids, Michigan but could not provide any more information. We thanked him and said we would keep in touch.

-4-

"Ain't no bus go to Dyer". That was the response Jim got when he ventured out the next day to find Nelson's car. Nelson had to have driven and the investigative nature of my husband would go to work. After stopping in and questioning the Sauk Village, Illinois and Dyer, Indiana Police Departments, he was directed to the Lake County Indiana Police where he was able to obtain the police report that said it all.

Sure enough Nelson said he took a bus. Jim drove around the gas station and the other businesses in the area and spotted an old red Toyota car with Illinois license plates parked across the street from the gas station at Smokers Den on 101st and Sheffield, Dyer. The car was unlocked and had a flat tire.

Jim spoke to the clerk, Karen, who informed him the car had been parked there for two or three days and they were about to call someone to have it towed. They were very nice and agreed to wait for him to come back and pick it up. Now we needed the keys, but first we needed to get a new tire. There was no spare in the trunk, only a few golf balls and a cane. Neither of the doors could be locked, and the windows wouldn't roll up. He had to leave it.

Jim looked into towing the car and the cost of storage. It was way too expensive and the towing company wanted the title, which meant that after 30 days of storage the car belonged to them if not picked up. We didn't have the title. So, later that morning after picking up a new tire, Jim and I went to the Security office to pick up both safe packets. We were told two men, probably in their 40's, had also been to Security looking for the safe packets to obtain the keys. Security already knew not to release them to anyone except the guardians. Thank goodness.

We signed out the packets, put the keys in our pockets and deposited the remaining items in the North Campus hospital safe. We then went back to pick up the car. A Will County police officer, who was passing by, helped Jim to change the tire. Now…where would we park the car? We decided the best and safest place would be the hospital parking lot. So be it.

Upon returning to the hospital, two men were waiting for us and wanted the safe packets and Nelson's keys to have the car towed. One man introduced himself as Nelson's nephew. We explained our position as appointed guardians for Nelson and explained the VAS Program. Upon further speaking with the first man, he told us he was a nephew-in-law. (He actually was the son of the sister of Nelson's deceased brother, Charles's third wife. Not a blood relative. We were to find this out at a later time.) I had the feeling we accomplished everything we needed to do at just about the right time, and also that we were the protectors of something, but not sure of what.

The second man was a friend of the first and rather insistent about gaining possession of Nelson's belongings. We again explained our position regarding the guardianship, the court system and our responsibility to Nelson. Neither seemed to realize the severity of Nelson's condition and when I questioned them about family members, they stated they only knew of Nelson's sister, Ruth, and the only time anyone called was if they wanted something. They insisted they could care for Nelson if they had his keys. By this time, the case manager, Mike Wertz, introduced himself and I again explained everything to them. I said, "Hey, you guys, come up with a treatment plan, a care plan to demonstrate how you will care for this man, where he will live, who will give him his medication, monitor his well being, keep him safe, and then present this to the Court." I had a bad feeling about this situation, but for now we were in control.

In the meantime we had some consents to sign for a surgical procedure to be performed on Nelson, a spinal tap and an HIV test to be done in the A.M. This part always caused me a little anxiety. I always had to ask myself if this was necessary and would I do this for a family member? Yes, I would.

The next day the Floor Nurse called to say Nelson tolerated the procedure well, and the results were negative.

-5-

The following day Jim and I drove to Chicago and drove past the "Hair Affair" barber shop on 95th St. It was open and doing business. We drove back down Cottage Grove to the barber shop on 79th St., Prince's. Naturally it was closed and we could see mail piled up in between the storm door. It was a strange feeling to be driving up and down the streets of my old neighborhood. This would have been in the 1940's and 50's. I guessed that Prince's Barber Shop had been there since the early 60's. At that time there was much racial turmoil on the South Side of Chicago. The schools, Hirsch High School where I attended, South Shore High School, on the streets and the parks, Grand Crossing, Calumet and Rainbow Beach, were all in unrest.

We were just kids, plain ordinary kids. We certainly didn't have Prejudice 101 in school or in Chatham Fields Lutheran Church where I was confirmed, but there were riots and racial upheaval.

My Dad's store was now a cellular phone shop. The Walgreen's across the street was gone. The Chatham bowling alley where I spent good times with my Dad or with my friends was gone. I wondered if the long dark staircase leading down to the alley was still there. There was no reset button, there were "pin boys" sitting up on a shelf waiting to stand up the pins. On Evans Ave. there had been a millinery shop where my Mother bought her hats. My dentist was in the building above Walgreen's. I remember a doctor's office, but you didn't go, that was when the doctors made house calls.

Around the corner on 79th and Cottage Grove was the Chatham Restaurant, where my friends and I would stop after school for a Cherry Coke or a Green River. That was where my father caught me smoking; it was not a good day. Remember "Sen-Sen"? You sucked on it so your breath didn't smell like cigarettes, but it didn't work. Around the corner on 80th and Evans Ave. sat a plain car with a uniformed police officer sitting inside. He was there to avert any trouble that might arise. The first black family had crossed 79th St. and lived in that apartment building.

Further down the street was Don's for hamburgers and fries, John's Pizza Parlor, 25¢ for an individual cheese and sausage pizza, not a slice but a whole pizza, Heinemann's Bakery, the Jewel Food store, the Hi Lo grocers, the Rhodes Theater on the corner of 79th and St. Lawrence, the penny candy store across from the show, Saturday all day cartoon and features, the carnival that came every summer, always something to do. There was Woolworth's 5 and 10, with the overhead music playing, which was the first time I heard Elvis's Heartbreak Hotel. Good memories not to be forgotten, but looking back, a little dimmed with time. Can you ever really go back? Yes, yes, you can, and I will. We'll be back with the keys to investigate the barber shop and talk with the shopkeepers along the street. Someone must know Nelson.

Later that afternoon we spoke with Mike Wertz, Nelson's case manager, about his continued treatment and discharge planning with the focus on a total care facility, probable nursing home placement. Here our support and recommendations from the VAS

Program were needed and accepted. We would physically have to check them out.

We next visited with Nelson and told him we had been in his neighborhood, 79th St. "Oh, that's nice, well I've been flying all day. You know those whirly birds keep you going in circles." Okay, let's try the weather. I said, "You know Nelson, it's a nice day for golf." "Yes," he said, "I'd like to get some time in before the weather turns." I asked about his handicap. "Oh, I haven't played in years, too busy." I asked, "Busy doing what?" "This and that," he said. He always smiled when speaking, and he had a twinkle in his eye that reminded me of the Cheshire cat. What a sweetie.

I took another look at his chart. There was a business card attached to his face sheet. He had had a visitor named Richard Douglas who left his card with address and phone number… Command Sergeant Major U.S. Army Retired. We would definitely be in touch.

-6-

When we returned to Chicago a day later, a very cold November day, we stood in front of Prince's Barber Shop and wondered where to start. The store next door to Nelson's was a beauty shop. There we introduced ourselves to Yamah, the owner and beautician, a very lovely young Nigerian woman. We assured her that Nelson was safe and explained our role as his guardians. She told us she saw Nelson on October 29th, a Saturday, and that he had been barbering that day. She hadn't seen him since and was concerned. She told us Nelson had been cutting hair daily and they spoke every day but he was, "a very private man who never spoke about anything personal". She gave us the phone number of a man that had been asking about Nelson and was also concerned. Yamah called him and he came right away. This was Tyrone Jordan, the police officer whose name was found in Nelson's wallet. He said he and his family have been friends with Nelson for many years. They all knew him as "Junior". Since Yamah's shop was in the same building, we asked her for the landlord's name and number to call him regarding Nelson's rent and living conditions, if known. This was another duty of the guardian, to make sure the monetary responsibilities were not overlooked so as not to be in arrears.

Tyrone asked us if we would like to walk down the street to meet Joyce at 624 E. 79th St., Joyce's Barber Shop. She was a friend of Nelson's. Meeting Joyce was delightful. She was a pretty lady who hugged both of us and whispered a prayer of gratitude, thanking God that Nelson was all right.

Again, we heard the phrase, "he was private". She also said that the past few weeks she thought Nelson was getting a little confused. She had spoken with him often and thought about asking him about his family, but never did. Joyce was sure Nelson stayed in the back of his shop. We planned to return the next day to check out the shop. We thanked Joyce and Tyrone and promised to keep them informed of Nelson's condition. They had our name and phone number.

In the meantime it was Veteran's Day. We stopped and bought a small flag, took it to the hospital and gave it to Nelson. We knew he was a veteran and had served in the Army. "I walked my post in a military manner." That was his answer to our questions about his service time. It seemed to me he tried so hard and deliberated so carefully with each answer, still smiling and holding on to my hand tightly, but just not sure exactly where the answer was.

Did he really not know or was he so used to not saying anything about himself? Oh, Nelson, what have you locked up inside, and how will I get to it?

-7-

Inventory, an itemized list of current assets, a catalog of the property of an individual, a list of goods on hand, the quantity of goods or materials on hand. This was the definition of inventory, but in no way prepared us for Nelson's shop. The keys, we had them, we had a lot of keys and it took a while to find which one fit the door for Prince's Barber Shop. Joyce was with us, she had walked down from her shop when she saw us coming down the street. I guess it wasn't hard. We kind of stuck out, and I thought Joyce was a little protective for Nelson's sake. But I still felt right in my old neighborhood.

I had an eerie feeling as we entered the shop, like we were interfering, trespassing, snooping and about to invade someone's privacy. But, that was what we did, and it was necessary to gather any information that would help us find out more about Nelson and hopefully find some family. The shop was neat and clean, everything was in order and ready for the next day's business. There were four leather barber chairs, all with clean towels draped over the arms, like Nelson had been expecting to open the next day. Four leather shoe shine chairs stood ready, a television, and casual chairs for waiting customers lined against the wall. The other wall had a large cabinet filled with numerous shampoos and other hair care products neatly displayed on the shelves. Inside the drawers were sugar, salt and pepper packets from fast food places…a lot of packets. Next to the cabinet was a Pepsi-Cola machine with a price of 15¢ a bottle, no bottles, but there were cans of pop inside. On a shelf was a can of

Comet and a rag ready for use. In one corner was a small table and chair which I thought might have been used for manicures at one time. It didn't look like it had been used for a while. We casually walked around; this was a nice little shop. Nelson went for a ride in his car, never to return. Sadness crept over me. Don't ask me why but I watered the plants. I said a prayer for all of us.

Photo's of "Prince's Barber Shop"

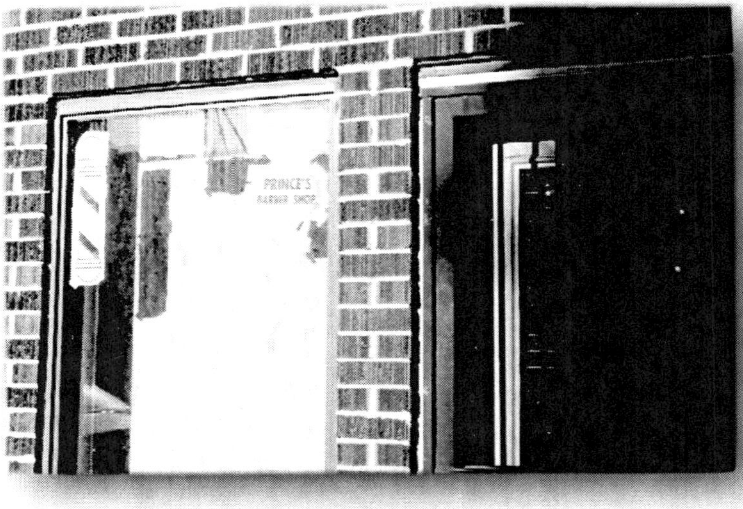

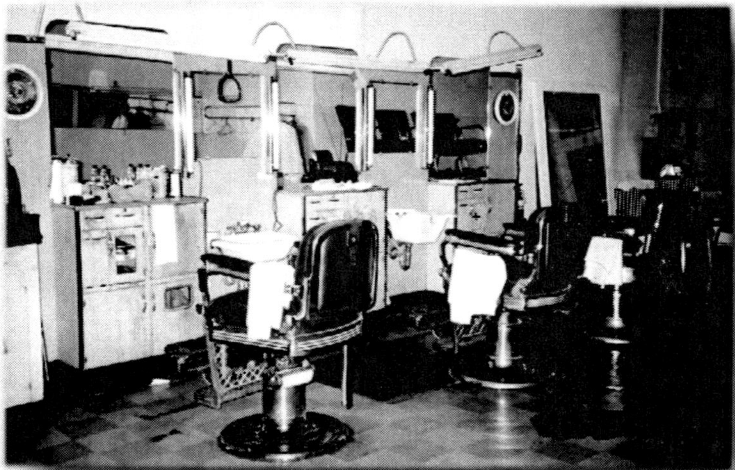

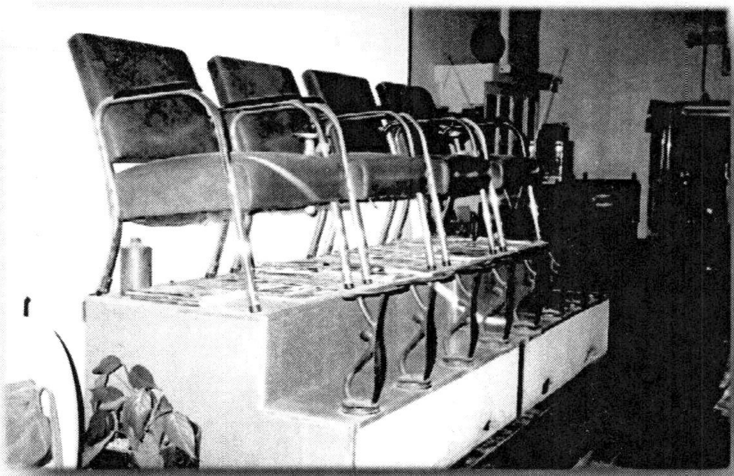

We walked toward the back hallway where there were two doors, both locked and more keys needed. Wait! I grabbed Jim's arm, jammed in the crack between the door and molding was a toothpick. Nelson would know if anyone entered. As we opened the door, the toothpick dropped to the floor and all three of us gasped! We stood there in awe; finally Jim said "let's take this slow". The first room was filled floor to ceiling with clutter. One double bed, one pillow, and half of the bed filled with papers, plastic bags, a TV set, clothing and mail, opened and unopened, no sheets or blankets which was hardly conducive to a good night of sleep. We were overwhelmed. One light bulb hung from the ceiling by what looked like an extension cord. There were lamps but none were in working order. The furniture appeared to be antique, maybe from the 40's or earlier. Behind the door was a chair filled with more mail, shoe boxes crammed with papers and some with shoes never worn. The dresser drawers were so crammed with stuff you were unable to close them. There was clothing from mail order stores that had never been opened. Socks, underwear, and shirts were still in the wrappers. On top were stacks of envelopes all with money in them, also bills and more bills. Upon close inspection these were found to be old bills already paid from years ago. Across the room atop the upright dresser were stacks of boxed unused checks about 18 total, unopened. A doorway was open between rooms and in the second room there was a small kitchen area, milk and juices in the refrigerator, boxes of cereal, cleaning supplies and on the corner of a small cluttered kitchen table were bottles of medication (diabetes, blood pressure, diuretics, and pain pills). The dates were all old with medication still in the bottles. Nelson had not been taking his medicine for a long time. His closet was full with old clothing, mostly white barber shop garb, and no outer wear like winter coats, scarves, gloves or boots. A lot of shoes and more boxes of old receipts, I mean old, from the 60's. In both rooms the floors were covered with papers, clothing, plastic bags and it was difficult to walk and not step on something. Behind the door in the second room were three sets of golf clubs and many, many boxes of golf balls and golf tees. I really felt like a trespasser now. Quite a difference from the barber shop itself, which was very neat and clean. We gathered up the envelopes we thought were the most current bills, bank statements, checkbooks, the envelopes with money and rolls of coins from the barber shop itself. I was a little uncomfortable that Joyce had to see how her friend had been living.

Did Nelson really live here? If so what did he wear, and where were his clothes? He must stay somewhere else. How sad! Was Nelson a packrat, a clutterer or a hoarder? Whichever he was, no wonder the toothpick, and the money just lying around loose. I was so glad we were the keeper of his keys and we were beginning to realize the importance of them.

-8-

Hoarding…people who tend to hoard usually feel a need to save and stock up on items that most people would consider throwing out. Hoarding creates such cramped living conditions it may be difficult to move around the room. Hoarders tend to form attachments to possessions rather than people and these possessions can become a source of comfort for them, and usually have a special meaning. They become preoccupied with their clutter and refuse to throw anything away; it just keeps piling up.

Somehow, with Nelson, he was able to contain all this mess without it spilling into the barber shop or impairing his daily activities in the shop. It appeared that most of the belongings had a purpose at one time.

For instance the receipts and bank statements…it wasn't just junk. Well, maybe it was and again maybe he was just a packrat and did not necessarily have a psychiatric disorder. Quite frankly, maybe it was just none of our business.

-9-

We now had what we thought was the most recent mail. Bank statements, checks, letters, cards, cash from the back of Nelson's barber shop were spread out over our entire family room. Where to start? First thing we had to do was to open a bank account for him in order to have his bills paid. We had to change his mailing address with the Post Office to have his mail sent to St. Margaret Mercy in Hammond, Indiana. VAS would help us with this.

In Nelson's wallet were a lot of old business cards with names of insurance companies, brokers and lawyers, and when Jim called them they were so outdated no one knew anything about them or of Nelson, except two.

Tenninga–Bergstrom was one. Robert Lofton was the sales

representative and most helpful. Nelson rented three garages to store his automobiles, and was up to date with payments. He had been renting these garages for over 30 years. One auto was stored in a garage at 111th S. Longwood Dr. and the other two at 616 E.79th St. In the 111th St. garage was a 1977 Volkswagen van and 79th St. was a 1969 Oldsmobile sedan and a 1982 Toyota Corolla. The Toyota was the car we had parked in the hospital lot. Mr. Lofton gave Jim the name and phone number of Joey, the maintenance man, who could help Jim open up the garages.

The second one was the Allstate Insurance Co. in Palos Hills. What was he doing way out there? They held the insurance policies for all three autos, all currently paid and up to date. These were two companies we surely would have to keep paying. My husband was an excellent detective! "Carry on," I said.

In the meantime I spent my days with Nelson. He was still in the St. Margaret Mercy Hospital in Dyer. I would question him about his family; he was still oriented to self only and tended to confabulate. We always held hands and he would smile at me and tell me how glad he was to have me there. Gradually he told me he was born in Tennessee, had a brother named Charles and a half sister named Ruth. He never married and had no children. He said maybe Charles had a son but was not sure of his name. I asked him if he had a nephew, maybe someone who called him 'Uncle' or 'Unk'. "No, No," he said with a tinge of anger. "No, nobody calls me Unk." That was a start, maybe I could piece together some of these names from his papers we had brought home.

Each day in the hospital friends visited Nelson. If I didn't happen to be there, they were told by the nursing staff to call me at home, which they did, or to leave their name and I would call them. Richard Douglas was apparently the designated visitor for Nelson's golfing friends and he took the job seriously. These friends were very devoted but with each one it was always the same. They knew him for over 40 years but they didn't really know him, and certainly not much about his personal life. "He was a private person." Duh….And I thought men talked a lot, especially in the barber shop. I guess it's not like the beauty shop. Most of these visitors were his customers and they all really cared about him. It was good to talk with them.

Nelson didn't look too good to me. I would continue to speak with the Drs.

and staff. He wasn't too compliant with PT or OT, O2 was intermittent when he chose to keep the nasal canula on. Possibly he had had a 2nd degree CVA. His right eye had a slight droop and was teary for which he had been getting eye drops. A culture had been done which was negative. The right corner of his mouth had a drool. His pupils were equal, a little slow to react but hand grasps were strong. He continued on the heart monitor and vital signs were within normal, thanks to the medication. Diabetes was unstable, there again medication was needed and helped. His appetite was pretty good, but he certainly hadn't been caring for himself for a long time. Nelson had a way of smiling, always cheerful and telling you not to worry. "I'm all right," he would say.

I don't know if he believed it or not, but I didn't believe it. I was worried. Dear God, help us find his family.

At times it was so overwhelming, small scraps of paper crammed into envelopes, an old phone book with numbers in Tennessee and Michigan. We called as many as we could but no one knew him. I can remember an old friend of mine telling me, "You just need to find ONE name or person that would know." On an old insurance paper there were four names, Joseph R. Anderson, Ruth Williams, Sharon A. Anderson and Michael J. Anderson. Okay, let's start.

Meanwhile Jim was hot on the trail of a few banks, investment companies and the landlord of Nelson's barber shop. From here on we would definitely need the guidance of the VAS Program and the use of our credentials. The Wolen-Levin Realtor on East 55th St. was the landlord and told Jim that Nelson had a monthly lease that he had since 1983. It was up to date on payment. Did he buy it from Prince and never change the name? More questions.

One of the many keys we had appeared to be for a P.O. Box and most of Nelson's mail that we retrieved had a P.O. Box number on them. This made sense since he had worked for the U.S. Postal Service for many years. So, off we went to the nearest Post Office on 79th and Cottage Grove. There we were told by the Postmaster that his key was for the main office on Clark St. downtown Chicago. That would be a day trip….another day.

I have a son, David Ainley, who is an attorney in Chicago, and through public records he was able to find that Nelson owned the building on 95th St. It had one apartment and the barber shop,

Hair Affair. He bought it in 1998 from Hawkeye Investment Co. out of Pa. after his brother Charles died and paid $120,000 cash. Taxes were paid up to date and no mortgage. Wow!

-10-

"Please find a very, very nice home," this was our request to Mike Wertz, Nelson's case manager. Based on bank statements, financial records and stock certificates, we were beginning to get the picture that Nelson was able to afford the best of care which he needed 24/7. We would have preferred to keep him close to our home in Dyer but his friends were all from Chicago and we thought it would be best. In hind sight maybe not, we probably could have avoided some problems with the nephew-in-law.

It isn't easy choosing a nursing home, especially in an area you are not familiar with, so you go and see each one and inspect them yourself. Officer Jordan suggested Montgomery Place, 5500 South Shore Dr., but they were filled so we put Nelson's name on the waiting list. The internet was helpful since they listed accreditation information and any infractions the home may have incurred, but when it came down to choosing, truthfully, your nose gave you the best answer. So we picked one, completed the paperwork, which consisted of our credentials, the court papers, guardian papers, Nelson's finances, which we had to guarantee, and all the guidelines, which we had to sign.

We then contacted Mike Wertz to assist and make arrangements for the transfer to Washington Heights on W. 95th St. in Chicago. Meanwhile Jim continued the search for assets, and I for family members. Jim said Nelson was like a little squirrel that buried assets in all different places and in all probability did not remember where everything was because a lot of his accounts had no recent activity, some for years. We were hopeful that something would have a beneficiary listed but so far none did.

Mr. Douglas, Nelson's friend, kept in touch almost daily and remembered golfing with Nelson in Iowa and thought maybe Nelson had grown up there. Here we go, another avenue and back to the internet, to look up the family names I had. First Ruth Williams, a half sister to Nelson, by his father, prior to marrying his mother.

Nelson was born in Nashville, Tennessee and brother, Charles, born in Appalachia Wise, Virginia. I did remember seeing papers with that name and also a school reunion program from Virginia. Jim was working with H&R Block and Morgan Stanley regarding beneficiaries and came across a Certificate of Deposit due for renewal from Bank One worth a large sum of money. During this period of discovery it was important that we maintain strict confidentiality and we were becoming excited about what we were finding.

From past experience with cases, ours and other volunteer's cases, most folks were without funds. As always, we utilized the expertise of VAS to guide us. Continuing to gain a rapport with Nelson was a pleasure too. He remained oriented to person only and during our conversations he seemed to really try to please me and answer my questions, searching for the words that wouldn't come but always with a smile. I believed a lot was confabulation and he had so much locked up inside. He would look at me and say, "Well, you know." I'd wait and wait, and he'd smile. The end. He had a cute laugh. I never was sure if he was laughing at me or with me.

I began getting him ready to be transferred to the nursing home; washed his clothes, the ones he had been found in and shaved him every day. It would be soon. Medically, more tests were being performed (stomach x-ray and bone scan) and an infectious disease physician was seeing him for an elevated white count. His circulation was poor; oxygen would be continued, along with insulin and his other medications.

Prayers, oh boy, we all needed them.

-11-

We took a trip to Chicago to the main Post Office and picked up mail from Nelson's P.O. Box, turned in the key and had his mail for 79th St. and 95th St. forwarded to St. Margaret Mercy Hospital care of VAS. Even though we produced our court papers and credentials, it took some time. The supervisor gave us a phone number to call regarding beneficiaries for Nelson's postal retirement; this was much appreciated.

Standing on the corner of Clark and Adams, we surveyed the corners. This was Nelson's domain. H&R Block, Chase and LaSalle Banks, all had accounts for Mr. A. Prior to our meeting with H&R Block, all of our papers had been faxed by VAS so our transactions went smoothly. During our meeting with the representative, he informed us there had been no activity on Nelson's accounts in over three years and no beneficiaries were listed. That was not good but seemed to be in keeping with Nelson's style.

At home the Utilization Nurse, Sue Fluga, from St. Margaret's, phoned to tell us that Nelson's tests were completed and all negative. All the hospital staff had been so pleasant and accommodating regarding our guardianship and Nelson's well being. Again we were thankful, and it was a blessing to have Nelson in Dyer. That evening the hospital supervisor (also my supervisor at work), Thad Stutler, received a phone call from Sharon A. Osborne and Michael J. Anderson, seeking information about their uncle, Nelson J. Anderson. Thad took their phone numbers and we promptly returned their calls. Thank you Thad! We had found a nephew and a niece!

Sharon apparently had been calling Nelson at the shop and no answer, so she called Michael to stop by the shop. When he found it closed, he asked around and was told Nelson was in St. Margaret Mercy Hospital in Dyer. Michael was Nelson's brother Charles' son and Sharon was Charles' daughter by a prior relationship. Michael lives in Chicago and Sharon in Maryland. They told us of Nelson's half sister, Ruth Williams, who also lived in Chicago. She was Nelson's father's daughter prior to marrying his mother. They truly were related. Wow, this was exciting! I couldn't wait to tell Nelson. Hopefully these names would spark some memory or recognition. It didn't seem to us that Michael or Sharon knew a lot more about Nelson, but we would certainly keep in touch with them. They were going to try to talk to Nelson on the phone. Good luck.

Visiting with Nelson was always a pleasure but that day was special. He was more alert and seemed happy to talk about family. If he did talk to either Michael or Sharon, he didn't remember it, but did go on to tell me about his grandmother, Lutie McKissack (his mother's mother), and wanted to talk about her as if he had seen her yesterday. He smiled from ear to ear, laughing and when he would begin a sentence he would start out with, "Well, you know." But then he was quiet and wouldn't say anything. I would try to redirect him and he would just smile. I'd be quiet for a while, and then start all over; that seemed to work better. He told me of a brother named Joseph and that he, Charles and Joseph grew up in Des Moines, Iowa. He talked about being in the Army, "maybe the Philippines," and of a half-sister named Ruth. He grinned from ear to ear telling me he didn't know about her until he was 21 years old. "Isn't that funny," he said and laughed. "Nope, no one else, anyone else would just be a walk-in, a wannabe, like the barber shop, a walk-in." So….the so called nephew-in-law that kept asking for the keys was no relative. Be watchful!

-12-

The transfer was complete and Nelson was settled in the nursing home, Washington Heights. It was a long term, skilled health care facility to protect his health, safety and well being on a 24/7 basis, since he was mentally and physically incapacitated.

That was very hard. I know that when he ventured out in his little red Toyota on Halloween eve after cutting hair all day long that this was not his plan. What happened so suddenly probably wasn't really so sudden, but I don't suppose he knew what to do or even who to trust. He was not used to telling people about himself.

Dementia, the word comes from a Latin word meaning "apart or away" plus "mind", a progressive decline in cognitive function. This is true; I have seen this in my work. A family would say, "But he/she was driving last week, shopping, nothing unusual." That sure scares you, doesn't it? Our denial systems work well.

In the meantime we had many calls to make to notify family and friends of his transfer. The move was closer for them and we knew he would have many visitors. Later that evening I called the nursing home to check on Nelson and to reiterate to the staff that Jim and I were the guardians and that no one was to take him out of the facility without our permission. The staff reassured me that Nelson was "getting used to them and they were getting used to him" and he was doing okay. However, the nurse did tell me that he kept falling asleep while being fed his dinner. This was new. He always fed himself in the hospital, even though his appetite wasn't real good.

Oh Nelson, don't give up. Did he know where he was? Was he afraid? I worried about this.

We had to return to the 79th St. Barber Shop for clothes. I needed to mark his name on all his belongings and return them as soon as possible. I hadn't done that since my kids were little but we didn't use markers; you had to sew on labels. Oh, the good memories.

A feeling of loneliness swept over me when we returned to the shop. I felt spooked. We never turned the lights on in the shop, only in the back rooms. We didn't want to have to open the door to anyone. The phone rang and scared the daylights out of me, but we didn't answer it. We continued to pick up papers, envelopes, whatever, anything we thought would help us to continue with our quest to learn more about Nelson.

The sense of responsibility was always with us. I felt so intrusive.

Of the clothes I took, many shirts and slacks were still in packages with tags on them. They were from mail order companies. I just wanted out of there as quickly as possible. I'd unpack them at home.

We walked down the street to Joyce's Barber Shop and she welcomed us with open arms. What a nice lady and so concerned. I knew I could count on her for whatever we needed. She said two friends of Nelson's told her that Nelson had a brother named Joseph, who was homeless, and Nelson would "take him in, clean him up and feed him." That's all they knew. How do you find a homeless person in Chicago? Nelson had a lot on his plate.

After we left Joyce's, we met Mr. Lofton from Tenninga-Bergstrom around the corner in the alley behind the barber shop to open the garages where Nelson kept the 1969 Oldsmobile. His little red Toyota remained in the hospital parking lot and each time I worked I could see it from the window of our staff lounge. Only one other person I worked with knew who it belonged to.

Jim and I continued to update Vanessa and an appointed attorney with our progress. As Limited Guardians this was essential and we always respected their input, well, Vanessa's anyway. We felt we could have paid Nelson's bills but we did have an obligation to report our progress to the court and the Judge in Hammond, which we did. Sadly, that same day we received a call from the nursing home to report that Nelson had become very short of breath, blood sugar was fluctuating and they were concerned. He was sent by ambulance and after an evaluation in the emergency room at Little Company of Mary Hospital, he was admitted with a diagnosis of pulmonary edema.

I spoke with the nurse at the hospital regarding his condition which was only fair. He was resting quietly but his blood sugar was very low and he was receiving I.V. fluids. I explained our role of guardianship and she gave me a privacy number for future calls. All the necessary court papers were on his chart from the nursing home. Then the calls began. The nephew-in-law called first saying, "This is a mess…I need the keys to find some papers…there is an insurance bill due for the 95th St. Barber Shop and I don't have the money." I wondered how he got the bill. I advised him to call VAS and notified him of Nelson's admission to the hospital, which he stated he already knew. He had been to the nursing home and they informed him. Regarding him and this situation, it truly was a court case now.

Next was a call from the niece, Sharon. The nephew-in-law had called her. (It was strange that all of a sudden he knew her name and phone number.) She seemed a little upset, stated her concern was about what Nelson's "wishes were regarding burial" and stated that his mother, Ruth McKissack, was buried in Detroit. She was from Nashville and had died in childbirth with Joseph. Nelson's brother, Charles, who was also her father, was buried in Chicago. He was a veteran of the Korean War. She continued to tell me that she had spoken to Nelson last night at the nursing home. She said he didn't like it there, he was angry and he hung up on her. "I'm not looking for anything, I just want my uncle to have his wishes granted and he always told me he would give me the Volkswagen bus." Well, that was interesting.

The next call was from Michael, the nephew, since Sharon had called him. He spoke quietly about his concerns regarding Joseph having "mental problems and homeless" and Sharon having "issues". Michael stated "no one except you and Jim are to care for Nelson right now." He said he would like the name of the attorney appointed to care for the finances. Again, I referred him to Vanessa at VAS. That was a real plus; I felt he had confidence in us and the VAS program.

Now, what about Nelson? Sister Christa from Little Company of Mary Hospital was calling regarding an order for a DNR.

-13-

"Grant his wishes," that's what Sharon said. Wouldn't it be wonderful if Nelson's wishes were known? If only we would find a Will or an Advance Directive telling what he wanted. An Advance Directive is a document that does grant your wishes. It must be done when you are of sound mind. It can be a request to/or not to have cardiopulmonary resuscitation (CPR) if your heart stops or you stop breathing in certain situations. This is fine if you have a terminal illness in the advanced stages but I'm having difficulty with this end of life stuff for someone else, when it is unclear as to his medical condition. I knew it was the right thing to do. We certainly didn't want Nelson to suffer or linger when there was no hope, but I wasn't ready to give a full DNR order either. There are Advance Directives with stipulations which would be better at this time.

God, please help us with this, I prayed. This part of limited guardianship was difficult; we'd have to sleep on it.

The following day…"Sorry it's my weekend to work; I'll meet you later." Jim went to the hospital to meet with pastoral care, Jim Rinhard and Marie Murphy, the case manager for Nelson, and discussed the DNR order. Jim reviewed the circumstances of how Nelson was found and the role of guardianship through the VAS Program and the courts. (Everyone we spoke with was in awe of the VAS Program.) Just at that time the nephew-in-law appeared at the nurse's station asking for Nelson's keys to the barber shop from the nursing staff stating, "He needed access to Nelson's finances to pay bills." *Again?*

Jim explained to him and to the staff that this was not possible, reiterating the role of guardianship and the responsibility that we had to abide by. He reassured the nephew-in-law and staff that the bills were being taken care of by the appointed attorney and gave him a name to contact with case and docket number. All of the concern at this time should be focused on Nelson and his well being which wasn't so good.

After work I met Jim at the hospital and we spoke with Dr. Sanet who explained that, "Nelson was in danger of losing his right foot due to diabetes and poor circulation." A surgeon was called in as a consult and we would see him in the A.M. After speaking further with the doctor, the DNR papers were signed, also release of information from

St. Margaret Mercy's Medical Records Department.

Visiting with Nelson was the same. "I'm all right" and a smile. He had O2 and IV fluids running and both wrists had soft restraints. The nurse told us Nelson had been up walking and was disoriented. He had climbed over the side rails and they were fearful of him falling. Nelson's right foot and lower leg were ischemic, pedal pulse was weak. This was not good. I untied his hands while we visited and he ate a very small amount of dinner.

"You can eat it," he said.

"Not me, hospital food, no, I'm peanut butter and jelly; I bring my lunch to work." I replied.

I tried feeding Nelson but he turned away. He didn't seem concerned or worried about anything and he wasn't oriented to time or place. I knew what was coming. I tried to reassure Nelson that we were doing the best we could and getting the best care for him. He would smile and hold my hand like he was trying to reassure me. Two visitors with the nephew-in-law had the nerve to have their names placed on the hospital face sheet of Nelson's chart to be called in case of emergency. We removed them. A privacy number was in place and if any friends called and asked about Nelson's condition, they were directed to call us, which they did.

One gentleman by the name of Mr. McCoy called. I remembered meeting him the first time we went to 79th St. when we were hauling out bags of Nelson's belongings. He stood in front of the barber shop watching us and finally asked about Nelson. He was very nicely dressed with a large gold 300 medal hanging from a gold chain. It was beautiful…bowling…maybe. Nelson was his barber and he thought that he lived on Champlain Ave., not behind the barber shop. I assured him we were taking good care of Nelson and we would keep in touch with him. I remember feeling kind of guilty and hoped Mr. McCoy didn't think we were robbers.

That evening, after a long day, Jim and I counted a lot of money and rolled up a lot of coins.

Bonnie and Clyde? No, the next day another trip to the hospital safe.

-14-

The vascular surgeon and cardiologist had completed their testing. After labs and dopplers, all the findings pointed to circulatory problems with probable amputation. I remembered Nelson had a cane in the trunk of his little Toyota. How long had this been going on? I didn't remember that anyone mentioned seeing him with a cane. More worries. This wasn't something that could wait. Nelson had no pedal pulse in the right foot which was becoming gangrenous, but he did have a pulse behind the right knee which was good. Vital signs were good and blood sugar was controlled. Surgery was definitely needed.

In the meantime some of Nelson's friends gave us input from their own experience with family members regarding nursing homes. Nelson was still on the waiting list for Montgomery House which was full, but they gave us referrals. Again we talked about placing him closer to our home but he needed his friends, especially now. We would look into a transfer to an Oak Lawn nursing/rehab facility after surgery and the social worker said she would help.

That day we met two more of Nelson's friends who came to visit, John Turner and John Johnson. They had played golf with him and also worked with him at the Post Office. Neither of them had remembered ever seeing Nelson walking with a cane but remembered him complaining of pain in his legs once in a while. Jim and I were so glad to have them there. We all tried to explain to Nelson the necessity of surgery to save his life. He just smiled and gave me his usual 'whatever' look and said, "I'm all right."

Confusion? This squeezed my heart. He didn't understand and nothing we could say would change that. His mind was locked and no key we had would open it.

I pulled back the covers and showed his friends the gangrenous right foot and silently said a prayer to myself for this sweet man who had to trust us.

Nelson did seem to know his visitors; he greeted them as if they were coming into his shop. He knew their names, and then told them that another one of their friend's had been sleeping in the chair next to him. I wondered at that time if he might be hallucinating. We'd have to call all his friends again to tell them about the surgery. Jim asked Nelson about the nephew-in-law and his role in Nelson's life. "He helps around and does odd jobs, my brother's wife's nephew, a wannabe, a hanger on. I take him out to breakfast on Sunday." Okay, he knew this, what else did he know? Maybe there was a small window right now. We pushed on. Nelson talked about a house in Des Moines, Iowa and said it was torn down. "Nobody lives there anymore." When asked if he had lived there at one time he said, "Well, you know," and then nothing. Again we brought up about the surgery, but no response; he just smiled. His outlook was certainly brighter than mine.

I had forgotten we had picked up his glasses from the nursing home and when I put them on him, he said, "Where did you get these?" I told him from his car and he said, "I must have had it parked in the yard on 63rd St." and he laughed. I'm sorry, but I had to laugh too. This little man was bringing me such sorrow but also much joy. Jim and I both signed the surgical and blood consent for amputation of Nelson's lower right leg. Surgery would be the next day.

This little guy had so many friends and they kept in touch on a daily basis. Mr. Douglas told us he had feelers out to find Nelson's family, especially his brother, Joseph. In their group of men, some had been together for 50 years. They were mostly in their 80's, but they would ask around. We certainly appreciated all of them.

We left the hospital and stopped at the Seaway Bank where Nelson had "a few" accounts and a safety deposit box. The bank was closed for the day and the officer stood inside the bank door with his hand on his firearm. (Again, did we look like Bonnie and Clyde?) He did not think this was funny. A very attractive lady graciously came to our rescue. Her name was Pat

McCreary, Senior Vice President and Cashier and she knew Nelson; he was a good customer. We showed her our court papers and we were in. Pat was so supportive and interested after we explained the Volunteer for Advocates Program. She, like the staff at the hospital, had never heard of such a program and wholeheartedly agreed that it was necessary. After reviewing Nelson's checking and savings accounts, we made an appointment to inventory the contents of the safety deposit box. Hopefully we would find a will.

When we returned home that evening, I returned a call from Muriel Glenn, a sweet-sounding friend of Nelson's. "We dated a little in 1954 but then I didn't see him for many years and we were reunited about three years ago. It was nothing personal, he just cut my hair. He was a packrat, a

Mr. Whipple. He cut hair for $8.00, that's why all his friends kept coming." Muriel went on to say Nelson had cut her hair about eight weeks before and it took him one and a half hours. She also said Nelson grew up in Des Moines, and had a friend Richard White who lived in Chicago who had known him in Iowa and I should call him. She also told me a friend of theirs confided in her that Nelson told him "one day in the shop he didn't know where he was or anything about it." Muriel knew that Nelson lived in the back of the shop and that at one time he had rented an apartment but gave it up. Another little bit of information to follow on another day.

-15-

A long day, but Nelson came through the surgery with flying colors. He received two pints of blood, and the surgeon and cardiologist were pleased. I was relieved! The surgery nurse told us Nelson kept asking her, "How are your sisters?" She was smitten with him, along with everyone else who met him. What a guy!

That evening Mr. Blair called, concerned about the surgery. He then asked me what I thought about the nephew-in-law. Apparently he told Mr. Blair that we would not give him access to the keys, or Nelson's personal property.

What did I think of him? I thought…good thing Nelson fell out in Indiana. At this point I was also feeling that our credibility was being undermined.

I reinforced to Mr. Blair that Nelson and all his property was safe under our guardianship and that all concerned parties had been notified by mail to respond to a "natural guardian interest". In other words if they could do a better job, prove it to the Lake Superior Court. "Well, you know" (as Nelson would say), sometimes you just get it right, and it feels good.

Nelson did well, never complained much of pain and would soon be ready for discharge to Manor Care nursing/ rehab home in Oak Lawn. His blood sugar continued to fluctuate, all his medications were continued and he was started on Plavix and aspirin. The left foot was still a concern, Doppler showed diminished circulation, second and third toes were dark, and amputation was probable in the future. This wasn't over yet.

Visiting with Nelson you'd never know he had his leg amputated the day before, and I'm not sure if he even knew. He was bright, smiled and grabbed my hand. In fact he was on the phone when we walked into his room. He didn't say much but listened and when he hung up, I asked him who he was talking to and he said laughingly, "Oh, I don't know." I told him I had spoken to Muriel. "Oh, you know Muriel?" "We went to Manila, Philippines School together." I asked him if he dated her. "We were young." I could never get a straight answer and I was to learn that nobody ever did.

I asked him about Richard White. "Yes, he lives in Chicago, kind of in the ocean; you walk out in the water." (Yes, Mr. White lived at Harbor Point.) Jim said to Nelson that Mr. White must have some money to live there. "Oh, he gets some green spots on his suit and he just brushes them off." Nelson sure gives you a pang in your heart. He fed himself lunch, even though he only ate a small amount.

We discussed with the nursing staff and case manager, Nelson's follow up care and options regarding a physician. We had been told his current doctor did not attend at Christ Hospital which was the closest to Manor Care; thus, he would be admitted under Dr. Mathur. This time after visiting I told Nelson we were going home to have dinner and feed the dog. He looked at me and said, "I had a dog named Fritz." He closed his eyes and had a smile on his face. He was remembering good times.

Jim called Mr. White and he said he and Nelson had been in the Army Medical Corps together in the Philippines for 14 months. He told Jim that Nelson was raised by two aunts in Nashville, Tennessee and then they moved to Des Moines, Iowa, where he graduated from high school. He said Nelson had gone to the University of Iowa to study dentistry but "did not adapt to the study program". He also told Jim there were doctors and dentists in the family (Nelson's father was a dentist), and there were relatives in Joliet who were cousins of his mother. A Dr. William Wilson, and his wife, Lenora, was a first cousin to "Doc Cheatham" who was a jazz great. Mr. White thought they all had died some years ago. He continued to say there was a library in Nashville named for one of Nelson's aunts. Further, Nelson graduated from Moler Barber College in Chicago and worked with his Uncle Prince. Mr. White and Nelson also worked together at the Post Office. Mr. White had a lot of information.

I was fascinated. I had to look into Nelson's background hoping it would help us and light a spark with Nelson so we could talk. Being an adoptee and having done a successful search to find my "roots", I had no doubt I could do this. Remember, I grew up in Chatham. My search was done the old fashioned way, many trips to the Newberry and Chicago Public Libraries pouring over old phone books, birth and death records, the courts, knocking on doors, phone calls, and mostly with the help of special friends. This time I had the Internet. Go girl!

-16-

Patience, that's what Seaway Bank granted me and Jim when we searched through Nelson's safe deposit box. Geri, a bank employee, sat with us and never once took her eyes off of us. It was an extra large box that was crammed full of papers, stock certificates, coins, paper money, jewelry, car titles and insurance papers with no beneficiaries, and no will.

Nelson was a packrat in his safe deposit box also. He kept everything, some important papers and some probably only dear to Nelson, like his invoice for his 1970 Volvo from Smith Chevrolet and his Saab key chain. But some were very important; namely, his birth certificate. He was born in Nashville, Tennessee in 1926 to his parents, Ruth and Nelson Anderson, race was Mulatto. His diploma was dated 1944 from his high school in Des Moines, Iowa. His Army roster papers from Fort Sheridan 1946, Apprentice Barber License 1952, and an old brown wallet that just happened to have $1330.00 in it. There must have been pin numbers from every bank in Chicago; even Continental Bank which I knew was out of business. I kept in my head, for whatever reason, the words on a small piece of paper that I had unfolded, Greenwood Cemetery. We might need that later.

Seaway Bank is located on 87th and Cottage Grove Avenues. Across the street in the 50's there had been a Walgreen Drugs and a Polk Brothers Appliance store. It seemed there were memories everywhere for me, thank you Nelson.

My friend, Cona Hickman Evans, and I would sit on that corner of 87th St.

making and selling pot holders, the ones made on a loom with rag yarn. Look in your potholder drawer. You may still have one since they wore like iron. Still friends after over 60 years, Cona and I often reminisce about, *'the good old days'* and they really were. We were full of life and fun. The years now are also good but in a different way since we are full of fun and age.

Cona & Joan

-17-

Vanessa Nathan from VAS and the appointed attorney were handling the legal and financial affairs. The court was satisfied with the establishment of an account at a Cook County bank to keep Nelson's bills paid and there was a recommendation to begin to set up a trust for Nelson's continued care. The Lake Superior Court Judge Don Stepanovich stated, "Classic, never had one like this." VAS was a wonderful program, applauded by everyone.

All pertinent family members and friends were notified of Nelson's transfer to Manor Care Nursing Home after almost three weeks of hospitalization. Nelson was really doing okay; stable, not good, not bad. He slept a lot and sometimes while visiting he would just close his eyes and you felt you were dismissed. He was tired, enough was enough. The transfer to the nursing home was smooth once we found his clothes. We had to track them down from the first nursing home which had sent them to a different Manor Care facility. This was all in a day's work.

We eventually signed the admission papers, met with the social worker and the physical therapist. The DNR was in place and hopefully wouldn't be needed, not on our watch anyway. This was December and over the next few days there were snowstorms, so driving to Oak Lawn was less frequent and I kept in touch with the staff by phone. Nelson was resistant to the PT and OT. He only wanted to stay in bed and sleep. His confusion varied but his attitude did not. If he didn't want to do something, he politely refused.

Our next visit was a week later and he didn't look good. I felt so sad for him. He was sitting up in the chair watching television with his roommate. We introduced ourselves to Jessie Cleveland, a soft spoken gentleman, about the same age as Nelson who was in the home for cardiac rehab. Each time we visited with Nelson we visited with Jessie too.

The pressure dressing was in place on Nelson's right stump and his left leg looked swollen with the second and third toes still dark. His right hand was tremulous and when they brought his lunch he couldn't seem to hold the fork, or even know what to do with it. I fed him since his appetite was poor. He wasn't his cheerful self, less talkative, no eye contact and he kept his head down and to one side. He spoke clearly but very slow. We still held hands. I shaved him and we kidded about him being the barber. "That's okay, you can do it."

Sure, me who gets nicks when shaving my legs. His voice was so soft and sweet. He trusted me.

I spoke with the nursing staff regarding his condition, reviewed his medications and asked that they please feed him each meal. I made a mental note to call the doctor. On the way home Jim and I stopped at the barber shop on 79th St. to pick up more clothes for Nelson and to be sure the mail was being diverted to St Margaret's.

It seemed there wasn't enough delivered to the hospital because we were getting calls regarding late bills. We certainly did not want Nelson's bills to be late; he had been so conscientious. Where was the "guardian of funds"? The answer I got was, "It takes time." You remember the old saying, "If you can't say anything nice, don't say anything at all." Well, we were almost to the "at all" part. We did pick up more to inventory, old tax forms and bank statements. We knew there was more of something.

Our next visit with Nelson found him in OT with the therapist. He looked much better and more alert. Kelli, the therapist, wanted Nelson to raise a bar over his head and bring it back down. He smiled at her and said, "If I do it, can I go back to bed?" We sat with Nelson and encouraged him to comply. He told Jim that he was "worried about his keys to the house" (the keys again). Jim reassured him that everything was safe and that no one could get to anything that belonged to him. Nelson grabbed Jim's hand and shook it, "thank you, and thank you". I sensed relief for him, but he still wouldn't raise the bar. Jim asked him if he felt anyone was taking advantage of him and Nelson said, "Yes, but I keep my doors locked, everything, everything locked." He went on to say, "This has been a peaceful week, no phones, no TV." I think he really meant it; he was at peace.

I always checked the visitors log at the front desk to see who had visited Nelson. Each Monday Joyce, Nelson's barber friend, had been there and I knew each time she shaved him. She was a loyal friend. I also checked his backside for any skin breakdown and his left foot. The second and third toes were still discolored...poor circulation. "I have a hole in each foot, right through to the bottom," he told me. I believe it bothered me more than him.

On the way home we stopped at the barber shop on 95th St. to speak with the nephew-in-law. He hadn't returned any of our calls. One of the barbers told us he wasn't there, that he was working. He asked us if we were related to Nelson. I said "do we look like it?" (Looking back, that was rude.) His answer was, "Nelson's father was white." (That was not true.) We explained we were Nelson's guardians and he went on to say that he knew the family for over 40 years and had worked for Nelson's brother, Charles. My thought was, so where were you two months ago when we were looking for family? We informed this barber, Eddie, of Nelson's whereabouts and condition. He said he knew nothing.

We also asked him if Nelson had any clothes in the apartment above and he answered "No."

I felt he was a little evasive and guarded. Why would that be? The nephew-in-law lived in the apartment above the shop. Did he pay rent?

-18-

"Where would they go?" This was the question asked by Nelson to his nephew, Michael Anderson. Michael spoke to Nelson on the phone and said Nelson was "worried about his customers." That sounded like a lucid thought and a valid concern. He was just as worried about them as they were about him.

Seems a lot of folks were worried. Michael and Sharon both knew Jim and I had been at the 95th St. barber shop. The nephew-in-law called them and he was worried. Michael said the nephew-in-law was worried about Nelson but also about himself. He said Sharon hit the ceiling when she thought the nephew-in-law would "get" the barber shop. What exactly were we dealing with?

An attorney, Mr. Brown, called Little Company of Mary Hospital asking questions about Nelson. The social worker, Maureen, obeying federal laws, gave him no information. She told us he told her he was hired by the nephew-in-law who wanted guardianship. She did not give him our name or phone number but gave us his number. I didn't call him, but made VAS aware of his call. We already knew his number!

Maybe I should start to worry. Remember, every concerned party already had all the information they needed from the court. What was going on? We were in the middle of something. Hey guys, we're just volunteers. In the meantime I talked with St. Margaret Security and again reminded them to keep an eye on Nelson's Toyota. We had to cover all the bases.

"That guy is too pushy; don't trust him. I saw him give a piece of paper to Nelson that he wanted him to sign. It looked like a check. I wouldn't trust him." This came from Nelson's roommate, Jessie. We appreciated Jessie; he seemed to keep an eye on Nelson. We knew he liked him. What's not to like? Jessie observed their visiting and said Nelson pulled away from the nephew-in-law and refused to speak to him.

Lunch was here…where were Nelson's teeth? He was sitting on them. I noted his backside had a small skin breakdown covered with a bio pad, he was diapered and too weak to turn himself. What's with the treatment here? Turn this man every two hours! Good nursing care was the preventive. Everyone heard about this! He was so fragile.

A visitor introduced himself to us as Melvin Bryant. Melvin said he was "so sad to see his friend this way." He called him, "Andy". There was questionable recognition on Nelson's part but he did smile at him. Melvin had worked, played golf and had his hair cut by "Andy". He was another good friend. During our visits with Nelson we would usually mention to him that he had been found in Dyer, Indiana and he would say, "That's when I had a headache." I would sometimes get the feeling he might have a slight recognition of that day but he never could put it together. He told Jim, "I went to White Sox Park to ride the elevator, no; I didn't have time to see the game." It was mostly just foolish talk which would end with "Well, you know." No, I didn't know, I wish I did. Administration notified us that Nelson was only in Medicare short term skilled care which was good for 90 days and only if he was cooperative. Nelson was uncooperative with OT and PT as he just wanted to stay in bed and sleep.

One time in OT, when asked to raise his arms and make a circle, he got so mad that he took his teeth out and threw them on the floor. I had to laugh (which didn't go over so well). I felt I had to defend him. My sweet Nelson wouldn't do that. I felt so bad for him. Where's the empathy? This was a business man from 79th St. Treat him with respect. I felt so sad I wanted to take him home. Now he was on the waiting list for long term.

I was getting too worked up over this so we went Christmas shopping for Nelson and Jessie. We bought them both new pajamas and decorated their room with a small Christmas tree. Merry Christmas boys!

A week later Jim had a cold so he stayed home and I went to visit Nelson alone. I walked into his room where a gentleman who introduced himself to me as Reverend Tommie Harris was there with the nephew-in-law. The nurse came in and addressed herself to both men saying, "If you want him discharged, you'll have to wait until I call the doctor for a discharge order." I was stunned, how dare them! I tried to calmly explain to the nephew-in-law and the Reverend that this would not be possible. I was not, however, as calm with the nurse. What would have happened if I hadn't arrived when I did? Nelson's chart was full of instructions from the court and the procedures that were expected to be followed regarding the guardianship. I sat with the nephew-in-law and the Reverend and both said, "Nelson would be better in his own surroundings with his friends." I couldn't have agreed more but this was not the way to do it. I said, "We are not your enemy, we are looking out for Nelson and his best interests." I was livid and shaking. The nephew-in-law left the room angry and the Reverend said to Nelson, "Eat your lunch so you can get back on your feet and take care of business. You need to hurry and get well so you can drive your car; you can't just leave it sit." I almost laughed in his face. What feet? How dare him! What had he been told? We had to talk in private. I didn't want Nelson to hear such nonsense. The Reverend said he had known Nelson for 12 years and that he lived behind the barber shop on 79th St. "No," he had never seen his living quarters. He did promise to find Joseph, Nelson's street brother, and to get me the name of Nelson's attorney and accountant. I told him I would appreciate it. (We never heard from him again.) The nephew-in law told me, "I'm not talking to you about this anymore, it's a mess."

Yes, he was right, it was a mess, but not for Nelson. We wouldn't let it be. I was wrong. The next evening, New Years Eve, an hour before the New Year, the nursing home called to say Nelson was being transferred to Christ Hospital in Oak Lawn due to shortness of breath and 30 minutes later the emergency room at Christ Hospital called to say Nelson had arrived.

-19-

New Years Day 2006, Christ Hospital

I spent the day with Nelson in the ER as we waited for a bed. He was admitted for pneumonia and pulmonary edema. He smiled when he saw me as he always did, but was slow to respond verbally. I told him he was in the hospital. I squeezed his hand and he squeezed mine. He was so frail. The ER had his history from the nursing home chart and I reviewed the guardianship court papers with the staff. He had oxygen by mask, antibiotics by I.V., a Foley catheter and a nitro drip.

I stayed with him until he was settled into his room and then went to the nursing home to pick up his glasses and his laundry. The home didn't provide laundry services so I had been doing it. I noticed it was less and less because he had been in a gown more than his clothes. Jessie, his roommate, was upset to know that Nelson was sick but it was he who called the nurses when he saw that Nelson was having trouble breathing. I thanked him and gave him a big hug.

Nelson was admitted under Dr. Mathur, who called us at home that evening. (A doctor who calls to update you on the patient. What a concept!) Dr. Mathur had called in consults, a pulmonologist, a cardiologist and an infectious disease physician. Nelson had a urinary tract infection along with the other problems. A nasal gastric tube had to be inserted because Nelson was either unable to or did not want to swallow. This was necessary for medications. The doctor also said that

Nelson responded to his name by opening his eyes but did not speak.

I made another round of calls to his friends. A very lovely lady by the name of Vesta Cole called me. She said she was a friend of Nelson's and Johnnie Johnson. She said "I've called and spoken to Nelson in every facility. He speaks clear but makes no sense; I'm worried about him." We will keep in touch with her. By now we had quite a list of friends to keep in touch with. We started a chain, starting with Richard Douglas.

The next time I saw Nelson I mentioned that I had spoken to Vesta. He said, "Nice girl, very thin, I worked at the Post Office with her." He remembered!

Nelson had the NG tube out and was taking his medications by mouth with a little applesauce. He seemed to be cooperating and was sitting up in bed. He didn't look so pale. I fed him a small amount of his lunch, and he tended to hold the food in his mouth and had to be reminded to swallow. His appetite was so bad, and he was so thin.

I asked him if I could call anyone for him. "No, call them when I'm out. I'm in a breeze now." Then I would hear, "Well, you know." No, I didn't know, I wish I did.

Jim and I would sit with him and try to make conversation and reinforce to him that we were taking care of everything for him. We would ask him if there was anything we could do for him. "I'm all right." He denied any pain, even though his bed sore was getting larger, his second and third toes on his left foot were necrotic, and he still smiled. How I loved that smile! He told us, "the days go by fast, I have nothing to do and that's fine." I asked him what he liked to do before he got sick. "A little of this, a little of that, and a little something in between." He was fun. I only wish I had known him before he got sick.

I spoke with the doctor and staff and Jim and I signed the consent papers for a right thorancentesis. This procedure was necessary to remove the fluid in his chest cavity.

In the meantime we were to learn that all those little scraps of paper found in his shop was money owed him for weekly chair rental at the 95th St. shop and the nephew-in-law was the collector. (I must admit the first time I saw these I thought Nelson was running a numbers game.) This money was Nelson's to pay his bills. Some of the bills were not getting paid. We knew this because we were still getting phone calls from creditors.

St. Margaret Hospital Security was anxious to tow the Toyota and the mail was not coming as fast as we thought it should.

Was it possible that somehow the mail was being sabotaged or was I paranoid?

A call to Tom Gryzbek, the CEO for St Margaret's, helped us to keep the car in the parking lot. I wasn't sure about the mail.

I kept checking with Montgomery Place and also talked with the administration at Hartsfield Village in Dyer; all had waiting lists for skilled care. I knew it was only a matter of time before Christ Hospital would be talking discharge. A surgeon had seen Nelson and said in his opinion surgery on the left foot was too risky for his condition. One liter of fluid had been removed from his chest. His breathing was better, but his circulation was poor.

He had emphysema, congestive heart failure, and still on antibiotics for pneumonia and UTI. A central line was put in to access the veins. Dr. Mathur confirmed Nelson's prognosis was, "not good, too many things wrong".

What else, I prayed?

And then, an answer by the name of Geraldine Wolfe, a friend of Nelson's from North Carolina.

-20-

"I was worried since I didn't get a Christmas card from him." The phone call came from Geraldine Wolfe. I wanted to hug her on the phone. She and Nelson had been friends since they were 21 years old and have kept in touch all these years. This was the answer to my prayers. I was so excited that I couldn't wait to meet her, and for Nelson to see her. She had been told by another friend that Nelson was in the hospital and that we were his guardians. We would meet her at the hospital.

Every one of Nelson's lady friends was beautiful. This was my thought when I first met Geraldine Wolfe. She was small in stature but big in personality, a bubbly affect and full of praise for her good friend Nelson. She loved him all these years. "We were properly introduced and he was wonderful to me and to my mother. We were good friends; he could trust us." Jerry had an apartment in Chicago and was living in North Carolina during the winter months. She was worried about him and here she was. I was so glad to meet her and grateful to have her here. She told us, "Yes, Nelson was born in Nashville, Tennessee, his mother died in childbirth when he was 5 years old; his father was a dentist who died when Nelson was 13, possibly from a self inflicted wound."

Jerry described Nelson as "secretive and stoic". I told her I felt so sorry for him, those were such important years in a young child's life. Jerry sat with Nelson and talked of old times. She thought Nelson recognized her, but he didn't say much, he just smiled. I had to laugh they were so cute together.

Jerry left the room for a minute and I said to Nelson, "Isn't this exciting? Jerry is here to see you." He said, "She's just waiting to be next." Whatever that meant, there went all my romantic notions. Nelson would be transferred back to the nursing home that evening. The I.V. and the Foley catheter were out but the oxygen was to continue and so was Jerry…Yahoo!

When we got home that evening there was a message from Tamara Tate, the daughter of Ruth Williams, Nelson's half sister. I returned her call and we had a very nice conversation. Tamara had not seen Nelson since she graduated from high school 30 years ago, but that memory was so important to her. Nelson had given her $50 for her graduation. I remembered seeing a thank you note from her among Nelson's belongings. She apparently was very important to Nelson also since he kept her card. Oh, yes, I know, he kept everything. Tamara said Nelson was so good to her mother, he was supposed to take her to lunch for her birthday in October but she never heard from him and didn't know what happened. She was a lovely young lady and we talked for quite a while. She will relay our conversation to her mother.

The next day Jim and I stopped at the Country Kitchen on 87th and Cottage Grove where the Post Office golfing fellows met every Wednesday morning. There we met Richard Douglas, John Turner and Scotty, and thanked them for their support. We gave them an update on Nelson's condition.

We left them and headed to 79th St. behind Nelson's shop to meet Mr. Lofton from the rental agency to check the car in one of the garages. There it was, the 1969 blue Oldsmobile; it looked brand new. Mr. Lofton told us the real estate agency never had to send Nelson a bill. He was always a month ahead with his payments for all three garages and he had been up to date before he was found in Indiana. How quickly this dementia must have progressed.

On to the nursing home where we found Nelson smiling, sitting up in bed listening to Jerry talk to him of their times together. *Sweet.* And again the nephew-in-law arrived confronting us with "Nelson belongs with him to eat better, sleep better and be up and around people he knows so he can come back to normal with his mind."

Oh, God, I wish it was that easy.

Jerry told me she would be coming to spend time with Nelson in the early morning to help with his A.M. care. I hoped she didn't feel intimidated. Oh, how I appreciated her. I had the feeling we should be at the nursing home more often. I was feeling uneasy and tired. I had a job, a home and a dog, "Duffy" who probably thought he was an orphan, and a 60 day report due to the court. Hard to believe it had only been two months. I really did appreciate Jerry and told her so.

On the way out of the nursing home an aide stopped me and said that the nephew-in-law had asked her, and she gave him, bus fare to get back home. This was not a good situation. Again I reinforced to the staff not to let anyone take Nelson out of this facility without our permission.

That evening I had a phone call from a lovely lady, Bernice Gibson, a first cousin of Nelson's. Bernice was a nurse, also a diabetic, who had her left leg amputated in June of 2005. Her father was Toussaint McKissack,

Nelson's uncle and brother to Prince McKissack, George, Edward and sister Estelle. Her grandmother was Tina (Tennie) McKissack. At one time they all lived together, including Nelson, with Tina and Grandmother Lutie Anderson in Nashville. She said the whole family was diabetic and that Prince also was an amputee who died about 30 years ago. This sounded like an amazing family.

-21-

Behind the scenes Vanessa, VAS Coordinator, was working with the attorney to apply for permanent guardianship in Cook County Illinois. for me and Jim, and we would gratefully accept. I really wanted to continue. As it was, our guardianship had been continued through the Court as was deemed necessary to protect Nelson's interests. A complete written inventory of Nelson's safe deposit box was needed, and new attorneys from Illinois needed to be appointed for Nelson's future care. Additional competency papers were also needed from the doctor. We weren't alone and we always felt that we and Nelson were receiving the best of care and advice.

Again we went to Seaway Bank on 87th and Cottage Grove. We arrived before the bank opened so decided to have breakfast across the street at The Pancake House where I had the best French toast ever. I would recommend it.

On the way out of the restaurant a man stood up from his booth and said to me, "Don't I know you? Weren't you my nurse?" Maybe.

The inventory at Seaway Bank took hours. We wrote everything down that was on every big and little piece of paper, six pages in all. Again Pat McCreary and her staff were so accommodating and truly concerned for Nelson's well being. They had never heard of a program like VAS and were very impressed with the functions and the dedication of the volunteers. We all hugged and prayed for Nelson. We were certainly meeting wonderful people on our adventure. I had jotted down a few more names and dates to help locate family members. I was ready to do some genealogy work.

Jim and I had an appointment with Dr. Mathur to discuss Nelson's condition and to have the doctor sign additional court papers. We met him at his office on West 63rd St., a block from Midway Airport. Dr. Mathur was so kind and understanding. We conveyed to him that our main concern, naturally, was for Nelson to be as comfortable as possible since his prognosis was so poor. I asked if an evaluation could be done for a prosthesis, just in case he were to rally. He agreed. In our discussion of nursing homes he stated, "most are good and if you're real lucky you may get one with an outstanding staff." We thanked him for his time and went on to visit Nelson.

This visit I had some information that I had obtained on the internet. I had joined *Ancestry.com* and was able to gain access to the1900 thru 1930 census. I mentioned the name Lutie (Nelson's grandmother). Nelson just beamed and smiled from ear to ear. "My Lutie, let's talk about her." The smile disappeared from his face and was replaced by a blank stare. I mentioned the name Lutie again. I was so excited, this time saying, "That was your grandmother, Grandma Lutie." "Yes" he said, and that was all. I felt he remembered but wanted to keep the memories to himself. You little stinker, all this work I've done and you won't share. I really believed he knew. After all, this was what he had been doing most of his life…not sharing.

Nelson had the sweetest smile and facial expressions. His eyes would kind of twinkle when he smiled. This time I mentioned his family, brothers Charles and Joseph, his parents Nelson and Ruth. The smile came back but he wouldn't or couldn't share. I really felt there had been a window of recognition. This is the sadness of dementia.

But he was still my buddy and we held hands until he dozed off to sleep. I wondered if he was dreaming.

Jim and I spoke with Maureen, Nelson's speech therapist, who said Nelson had difficulty swallowing at times even with the pureed and liquids so they were using 'thickem' to help, but his appetite was poor. Nelson does hold the food in his mouth and has to be encouraged to swallow. I was thankful that he still had his teeth. My experience with the elderly was that they often misplaced their dentures either putting them somewhere in their bed linens or leaving them on their meal trays. One time a co-worker and I went through the entire hospital breakfast garbage looking for a patient's dentures. Sure enough we found them…wrapped inside a paper napkin. It's the little things to be thankful for.

Two friends, Robert Ward and Neal Gillie, stopped to visit. He had worked with one of them at the Post Office and Nelson had been their barber. I woke Nelson and left them to visit. Nelson was always so good at making people think he knew who they were and he genuinely welcomed their company.

Later I tried to feed him lunch. He only ate a few spoonfuls and when I tried to encourage him to eat more he said, "I'm all right." I was to hear this phrase a lot. I helped the aide with bedside care, linen and diaper change, and sponge bath. I cleaned his dentures. He was so thin and his backside was not healing; this was a decubital ulcer (bedsore). Again I would ask him if he hurt and he always answered, "No, I'm all right." I didn't believe him anymore.

On the way home we decided to stop at a funeral parlor around the corner from Nelson's barber shop on Cottage Grove. As guardians we would be able to pre-plan funeral arrangements and knowing Nelson's finances as well as we did, we knew it was possible to pre-pay. I wanted it to be right. I was beginning to find pieces of his family history. It was our responsibility to make sure this would follow Nelson's wishes…as we thought he would choose, if he were able. We parked across the street in their parking lot and proceeded to cross. We stood in the middle of the street and noticed a gathering of people, presumably a funeral service, spilling out in front of the parlor and heard loud voices and shouting. All of a sudden, out of nowhere came sirens, traffic stopped, police cars, marked and unmarked, zoomed in, policemen running toward the crowd and there we stood in the middle of the street. *Bonnie and Clyde?* Nope, it wasn't us. Everything happened so fast…a lot of shouting and yelling angry words. We quickly ran back to our car and as fast as it happened, it unhappened. The crowd dispersed, the police left and so did we. It wasn't funny, but we had to laugh.

What the hell were we doing here? I do believe Nelson is a little bit too sedate and private for this type of excitement. Again in my head was that little piece of paper, Greenwood Cemetery. I must find them.

-22-

Jerry's visits to Nelson were so important to him and to me. She would see him in the morning and help feed him. Sometimes she brought him food that she had prepared at home, thinking it would help his dwindling appetite. She took such good care of him, and all the while, she talked of their past together. She brought spirituality into her conversation and always thanked God for their friendship. She spoke softly and kindly to him. Mostly he would just smile and agree with her.

He always had friends stopping in to see him and I knew that Joyce still came every Monday to visit and shave him. That afternoon Jim and I visited at lunchtime and Jim asked Nelson if he had eaten yet. "I went across the street to eat with that lady sitting over there." He smiled broadly, laughing and telling Jim what a wonderful time he had. Sounded to me like a guy thing. Bless his heart, you just wanted to hug him.

On his bedside table was a greeting card and I asked him if I could open it for him. It was from Ruth Williams. "That's my sister." He was right, Ruth was his sister, but there was no lady sitting in the room and he had not gone anywhere to eat.

I believe he was hallucinating. I fed him two bites of his lunch; "that's enough" he said. I would wait a few minutes and start over, another two bites. He would forget he had the first two but he eventually caught on and that was the end of lunch. When he rested he didn't appear to be in pain. He seemed at peace, and I'll bet he listened to every word Jerry spoke to him about the scriptures.

God was with him. He was with all of us.

Medically he was worse, but the oxygen nasal catheter spent more time on his forehead than his nose. His toes on the left foot were gangrenous; his butt was worse, but never a complaint, always a smile and a squeeze of my hand. We always asked him if he had any wishes or if we could do anything for him. "No, I'm all right." So I fed him ice cream and he ate every bit of it. What the hell.

-23-

Greenwood Cemetery, Nashville, Tennessee

I spoke with Norma who gladly shared all the information I needed. There was a family plot, Section #5, Simons Ave., Lot 213. I was overwhelmed with my find. It had been so easy. Hers was the name from that small piece of paper in Nelson's safe deposit box. And there it was. Nelson would never be alone again. We would make sure he would be buried with his family at Greenwood Cemetery in the family lot with Lutie Anderson, his grandmother. She was interred in 1950, the last to be buried in the family plot prior to Nelson.

Also buried in the family plot was Lutie Cheatham Wells Anderson, born 1864; Ruth Virgina McKissack

Anderson, born 1906, Nelson's mother, interred 1933 when Nelson was 5 years old; Nelson J. Anderson, Nelson's father, born 1901, interred 1940 when Nelson was 13; Nelson James Anderson, Nelson's grandfather, born 1866, interred 1904; Thomas Wells, Jr., a child, buried with Ruth in same grave; Thomas Wells, Sr., no year of death; Fred Wells interred 1939; Elizabeth Wilson – date unknown.

I was so proud of myself. I was to later learn that Nelson's cousin Adolphus Anthony "Doc" Cheatham also was buried in Greenwood Cemetery.

"Doc" was born in Nashville, Tennessee in 1905 and lived there until he moved to Chicago in 1926. He was a jazz trumpeter, played saxophone, sang, and was a bandleader. He played in some of the top jazz groups. The nickname "Doc" came after he chose not to follow his family's plans for him to be a pharmacist. His career blossomed. Over the years he toured and performed with Cab Calloway, Freddie Keppard, Claude Hopkins, Sammy Price, Herbie Mann, Benny Goodman, Louis Armstrong, Ma Rainey and many other famous musicians.

"Doc" won a Grammy in 1996 when he and Nicholas Payton recorded a CD for Verve Records. He continued touring and playing gigs until his death in 1997. He died 11 days before his 92nd birthday. You may read his book, "I Guess I'll Get the Papers and Go Home: The Life of Doc Cheatham."

(NOTE: All census information that follows was gathered from the internet)

<u>1900 census, Nashville, Tennessee</u>
In household:
Nelson J. Anderson, age 34, born 1866, school teacher (Nelson's grandfather)
Lizzie (Lutie), born 1864 (Nelson's grandmother)
Martha Wells, age 19
Fred Wells, age 18
Lizzie Wells, age 14
Jennie Anderson, age 3
(Lutie's children prior to marrying Nelson grandfather)

<u>1910 census, Nashville, Tennessee</u>
In household:
Lutie Anderson, age 46
Martha Wells Brown, age 30, daughter
(Martha graduated from Fisk University, Nashville and later became the first librarian at Tennessee A&L

State College. In 1949 the library was named The Martha Brown Memorial Library.)
Samuel H. Brown, age 43, teacher
Fred T. Wells, age 27, porter for Pullman Car
Elizabeth S. Wells, age 24, teacher
Jennie L. Anderson, age 13, student
Nelson J. Anderson, age 9, student
(Nelson's father)

<u>1920 census, Nashville, Tennessee</u>
In household:
Lutie Anderson, age 56
Martha M. Brown, age 40, widowed
Jennie Anderson, age 23
Nelson J. Anderson, age 19
(Nelson's father)

1930 census, Appalachia Wise, Virginia

In household:

Nelson J. Anderson, age 29, dentist (first black dentist in Appalachia)
Ruth V. Anderson, age 26
Nelson J. Anderson, Jr., age 3
Charles Anderson, age 1
(Joseph Anderson born 1933; his mother Ruth died in childbirth)

1910 U.S. census, Nashville, Tennessee

In household:

George McKissack, age 50 (Ruth, Nelson's mother's father, his grandfather)
Tennie McKissack (Tina), age 40 (Nelson's grandmother)
Toussaint McKissack, age 12, (Bernice Gibson's father)
George A. McKissack, age10
Prince H. McKissack, age 9

(Nelson's cousin that owned the barber shop)
Lula B. McKissack, age 7
Ruth V. McKissack, age 6
(Nelson's mother)
Clarence A. McKissack, age 4
Nathaniel R. McKissack, age 3
Edward O. McKissack, age 1-1/2
Anabela McKissack, age 90
(great –grandmother)

Father (3times removed): Ashanti Tribe West Africa
born estimated 1739 to1768;
died estimated 1793 to1853

Mother (3times removed): Ashanti Tribe West Africa born estimated 1748 to1771
died estimated 1793 to1859

Moses (2times removed): Ashanti Tribe, West Africa,
born 1790 and died August 26, 1865, Spring Hill, Tennessee

Moses was sold into slavery to William McKissack of North Carolina and became a carpenter. He married a Cherokee Indian, Mirian, and had 14 children. Moses' children continued in the building trade that was passed on and on down the McKissack lineage. Their architectural and engineering designed structures can be found at Vanderbilt University, Fisk University, Tennessee State University (The Martha Brown Memorial Library named for Nelson's aunt), Pearl High School, Capers Memorial Church and many more public buildings throughout the state of Tennessee. This established one of the oldest African American architectural firms in the United States. It is still in business today.

According to an article I read on line, in Nashville, Tennessee on July 26, 2005, First Lady Laura Bush attended a ceremony on "Preserve American Neighborhoods." During her speech she spoke of the educational system and the pride in the history of Nashville and the many stories of its entire people. Among them she mentioned the story of the McKissack Family and their contribution to the city.

I thought about all the little pieces of paper with names, addresses and phone numbers that Nelson had written down and wondered who they were. I'm sure he visited many on his lone car trips…family history…so delicate.

-24-

Nelson was always pleased to hear names of family members and this was helpful for me too in talking with him. We bonded well. I told him that I had been researching his family tree and mentioned the name Moses, a slave from Africa sold to William McKissack and he would be Nelson's great, great grandfather. He got so excited that I thought he was going to jump out of bed. He smiled, his eyes widened and he said, "Yes, yes." I said, "Yes, yes, what?" His mind closed too soon, but maybe for just a minute he had a good memory of his past history which I was finding fascinating.

Richard Douglas visited that afternoon. He saw how emaciated Nelson had become and was very concerned. Nelson had I.V. fluids running, he was dehydrated and weak. Jim took Mr. Douglas aside and discussed funeral arrangements. He told him about the incident on Cottage Grove and of our concerns for more serene surroundings. He gave us the name of Taylor Funeral Home on 79th St., said they had buried his mother and he was pleased and we were again thankful for all his help and support.

Two days later we had an appointment at the Taylor Funeral Home on 63 E. 79th St. It was very quiet with peaceful surroundings that seemed more like Nelson. We met Nicholas Taylor, the funeral director, and introduced ourselves. We showed him our court papers and explained our role as guardians to Nelson. I explained that Nelson had a barber shop a few blocks down the street. We came to pre-plan and pre-pay a funeral. Nicholas Taylor was kind and compassionate. He helped us choose a casket and we discussed the burial in Nashville. He phoned the Greenwood Cemetery and made pre-arrangements with a funeral director in Nashville. He promised to help us further, if we needed anything. He gave me his card which I would place in the front of Nelson's chart at the nursing home.

This truly had been a very difficult task. I hated to think of the day I wouldn't be visiting with Nelson.

We chose a Batesville casket, naturally, made in Indiana, model "Tiger Eye" with a copper exterior and outer burial container "Venetian". We ordered a monument marker with engraving and a shipping container to Tennessee. We thanked Nicholas and in our hearts we knew we would be seeing him soon.

That evening I called Ruth Williams, Nelson's 82 year old half sister to tell her about the arrangements and asked her if she had any requests or suggestions. We talked family and she told me about Aunt Martha, Aunt Elizabeth Adams, and Genevieve Shetter, Nelson's father's sisters who had raised him in Des Moines, Iowa. (Jim had found property that Nelson owned and had been paying taxes on in Polk County, Iowa on Wallace St. From the papers Jim found, we had the feeling there was more. In fact Jim always had the feeling that we had just scratched the surface.)

Ruth was a sweet lady to speak to on the phone. I would like to meet her in person.

Ruth told me about her children, Tamara Tate from Chicago, Harrison living in Milwaukee, and Manuel in Chicago. I thanked her for the card she sent to Nelson and reassured her Nelson knew it came from "my sister".

I wanted to talk with her more, to learn more about her and the family, but as guardians we still had our job to do and I felt we had accomplished so much already. I never dreamed that two years later I would want to write a book. Nelson's memory never left me.

On our next visit with Nelson I told him about my talk with his sister Ruth. "Well, you know, she made a remark to me," and he smiled. He seemed so pleased to hear her name. I just knew he had good memories; his mind wasn't a blank all the time. He had thoughts and feelings but he just wasn't able to articulate them.

Jerry was visiting, had fed him some yogurt and he was comfortable. He was taking small sips of water but not enough to hydrate so he still had I.V. fluids running. He never lost his smile or his good nature. She was a blessing to him.

After conferring with VAS and the attorney, we were told the funeral parlor would have a check next week. (That turned out to be one of those, "the check is in the mail" deals but Nicholas Taylor was trusting and understanding.) Then again, everyone we met was like that. But why should anyone worry? Our names, mine and Jim's, were on the "Charge for Services Selected", the "Illinois Consumers Guide to Pre-need Funeral and Burial Purchases", and the "Homesteaders Life Insurance Company." So, who's trusting and understanding? Duh!

-25-

So many unanswered questions, some loose ends, but time was running out and I thought we had the essential information we needed for Nelson's journey home. We had his family's support and enough information had been gathered on our part.

Nelson had family. We heard from the daughter-in-law of an aunt, Susie McKissack. His Uncle George's wife, Susie, was in a nursing home in Michigan. Her daughter-in-law, Shirley, told us of Dr. Willie T. and Lenora Wilson from Joliet. More family that cared for Nelson. Yet when I mentioned the Wilson's to Nelson, he told me they had died. I guess he knew more than they. We would take the rest of Nelson's needs "a day at a time".

Our subsequent visits went well. During one visit we met Michael Anderson, Nelson's nephew. We had been keeping in touch with him on a regular basis. It was nice to finally meet him. I wasn't sure if Nelson recognized him, I doubted it, but he was glad to see him. As I've said, Nelson always made everyone feel like he knew them. Maybe a little familiarity came through, I hoped. (After Michael's mother divorced his father Charles, she remarried and had two more children. Her name is now Mary David.)

I was glad Michael had family. He was a nice man, quiet with a friendly smile like his uncle. We told him our concern about the 95th St. barber shop that was owned by Nelson and that the rental was due each week for the barber chairs. As far as we knew it was not being paid. This was Nelson's money and could help with his medical bills.

Regretfully, Michael had no control over this and neither did we. Nelson, apparently listening to our conversation, sat upright and said "Where am I based?" "You're based right here with us," I told him. He was satisfied. Keep it simple.

Sometimes I would ask him if he remembered driving to Dyer and sleeping on the lawn. He would simply tell me, "I had a headache." Some days Nelson would refuse to take his medicine, he would sleep a lot which was a blessing and only eat and drink small amounts. He was so thin. I would help the nurse's aides with bathing and linen changes. I would say, "I don't know what's keeping him alive?" The aide would say, "his will". This made me think we should tend more to his spiritual needs.

I always felt we were missing something.

I discussed this with the staff and they said they would call a priest. (We knew he had been baptized Catholic but unsure if he belonged to a church.) Later that day a priest came and asked Nelson if he wanted communion and he said, "No, not today." The priest stayed and prayed hoping Nelson would chime in. Nelson smiled, the priest smiled, and that was that!

The next time we visited, Nelson was asleep. I softly spoke his name to wake him and as he laughed he said, "So nice to be aroused by you." I teased him and called him a flirt and we laughed. I fed him lunch, he ate better and drank part of a milk shake. He had been listening. *The angels were with him.*

I read a Valentine card to him that had been sent by Jerry, and asked him if he had ever been in love. "Only puppy." *That was sweet.* I knew the time was nearing when Jerry would leave to return to North Carolina. She needed some time to take care of business. She told me, "Leaving would be a hard decision." I was so grateful for her and I knew Nelson would miss her. Later Jerry came to say goodbye and we hugged. I hated to see her leave. I felt she didn't want to be here when Nelson passed; she denied this, but I knew. I didn't blame her, I had to respect this. Jerry called me Nelson's angel but she was the angel; they had such history. She always said we were "the angels given to Nelson at his most needed hour".

That afternoon Jerry went to the neighborhood Catholic Church, St. Louis De Montfort, the parish where the priest resided. She made a contribution and had prayers said for Nelson. She left a note for me on Nelson's bedside table. As I read it,

2 - 15 - 06

Hi Joan

Here is the priest information. I will leave a donation for him enroute home today

Never will I forget you and Jim's efforts in Nelson's behalf

I'll keep in touch from North Carolina

Love always
Jerry Wolfe

Jerry's Note

tears welled up in my eyes. She was an inspiration to all and I know she brought peace to Nelson whether he wanted it or not. She left on Saturday, February 15th. Jerry always ‘kept her light under her bucket’. This was a saying I heard once from my Swedish cousin Dorothy Dasbach also from Chatham, and it certainly applied to Jerry’s modesty. Mentioning Dorothy, I should also mention my other Swedish cousin from Chatham, Peg McCambridge. She’s 95 years young and lives in Dyer close to me. Both ladies are very important in my life.

We continued to field phone calls from friends and family. I would always tell Nelson about the calls and sometimes they came in on his phone in his room. I would hold the phone for him; he would listen but never talk. His expressions told me he was pleased. He truly liked people and the feelings he had were locked in his heart.

On one visit, Jim noticed Nelson wasn't wearing his watch. Staff told us Nelson had given it to the nephew-in-law. We discussed this with the administrator who gave us a lecture on "patient's rights". No, he was incompetent. Nelson was so nice he would give anything to anyone who asked.

That's what we were for; please let us make those decisions.

This was very frustrating. The little nurse's aide told me "I was there, I stayed out of it." I again reminded myself of the "keys". When I asked Nelson about his watch he told me he "lost it". I really had the feeling just by the look on his face and no eye contact that he knew he wasn't telling me the truth. There was always something.

He was very talkative this day. We laughed about his grandmother, his cousins, his time in the service. "Oh, I was in the Army with Richard from Burlington, Iowa. I was born in Tennessee, and he was from Iowa. I was with him on New Year's Eve two weeks ago." I asked him, "What year is it?" He said, "I told you two weeks ago, is that good enough?" He laughed. We both laughed. I just shook my head and he shook his head and we laughed again. I told him, "You have a wonderful family, very well educated." He smiled and said, "thank you".

In the meantime we found out that the mail was somehow being returned to sender and not to the hospital which meant Nelson's bills were not being paid. Where were his bank statements and checks going? The post office in Chicago had copied our licenses, our court papers, our guardianship papers, so how could this be? We also found out the nephew-in-law was sending FedEx envelopes to the hospital with 95th St. bills to be paid. Where's the red flag? An appointment was made with the Judge, but probably too late. As guardians we should have been able to pay the bills; we certainly knew more about them than anyone. Was I sounding a little possessive? I needed to remind myself that this guardianship was limited.

-26-

On February 22, 2005 Dr. Mathur called at 8:30A.M. Nelson was not responding, all systems were shutting down, his blood sugar was low and a glucose I.V. was running. The doctor thought he probably had an infection, his toes remained necrotic and his stump was becoming discolored, but he was too ill for surgery. We discussed quality of life and taking him to the hospital; both of us agreed he should remain in the nursing home. The DNR was still in place. I had one request. Please move Nelson to a private room for his dignity, and so as not to upset his roommate Jessie. We were on our way.

He opened his eyes, those beautiful greenish brown eyes, and he smiled. Jim was on one side and I on the other and we held his hands. "I'm all right, I'm fine, really." We talked about Suzie McKissack, "my aunt". She was on his mind again. I told him she would be 100 years old soon. "I'd like to see her," he said. I fed him a cup of ice cream; he sure loved his ice cream.

It just happened that Jessie was to be discharged that day. He had completed his cardiac rehab and would stay with his daughter. We were glad for him and that he would not know about Nelson; he watched over him so well. We hugged and wished him well. You know, I've always been a hugger.

That evening at 8:05 the nursing home called to let us know that Nelson passed on quietly in his sleep.

I knew he hadn't been alone and that the angels had come to take him home.

We cried. My first call was to Joyce. We cried and prayed for a wonderful man. The next call was to Jerry and we really cried. She lost a good friend. The nursing home had also notified Taylor Funeral Home. The remainder of the evening was spent on the phone with his family and friends, mostly by Jim as I was wiped out. We would make the necessary arrangements in the morning.

-27-

It was a cold February day in Chicago, windy and bleak; your soul is cold, damp to the bone. This was our day to plan a funeral service. As usual Nicholas Taylor was the perfect host, guiding us step by step toward our goal to celebrate Nelson's life.

We planned the service, Nicholas made calls to Greenwood Cemetery and the J.W. Adkin Funeral Parlor in Nashville. Nicholas made airline reservations for Nelson's body to be shipped from Chicago to Nashville after the funeral, and before he hung up the phone he suggested that if the director in Nashville should need to contact him, "just ask for Reverend Nicholas Taylor". Well that solved our next question of who would officiate the service and say the eulogy.

I believe Nicholas was being modest when he said he had never been asked to do a service before but, whom better than he? He knew everything we knew and it would be perfect; I just knew it. Nelson wouldn't have wanted a stranger and the priest that visited the nursing home didn't go over so well.

We went over the calendar and set the date and the time. The weekend was coming up and it was my weekend to work. (No, I'm not such a dedicated employee that I wouldn't call off, but not on the weekend, that's a no-no, and Monday from 3-11, I had to be there.)

And a repast, that was a must after the service. We knew how important the food element would have been to Nelson. Nicholas suggested Captain's Hard Times Restaurant which was a few blocks down the street. We went there with Nicholas and met Josephine Wade, who planned the menu with us. When we were introduced as guardians, she quickly ran to a file cabinet and said,

"Here, I've got unpaid bills that are still in the probate court system and this one is over a year old." We just stood and looked at her, laughed and told her not to worry while we decided who would pay the bill.

Nicholas said he would and we said we would. It was comical. Finally it was decided the tab would be added to the funeral bill. Nelson would pay for it. That being decided the menu was finalized. It already had a festive flavor to it. We thanked Josephine for her help and reassured her again the bill would be paid. I glanced back at Nicholas and he winked. I thought 'all these folks trusted us, everywhere we went, and all the people we met; what a nice neighborhood I grew up in.'

Nicholas gave us a to-do list and we set out to accomplish it. First, we stopped at Joyce's barber shop for hugs. She unexpectedly presented us with a beautiful plant and a very thoughtful card expressing her thanks to us. We were the ones to be thankful to her and to all of Nelson's friends for their support and friendship, not only to Nelson, but also to us. Because of them the day was brighter. We discussed the funeral arrangements with Joyce and she suggested a funeral program instead of funeral cards. She said "folks like to remember".

Again, we had to stop at Nelson's barber shop; I hoped it was the last time. I still had thoughts of how he had left the shop that Halloween Eve and drove his little red Toyota to Dyer, Indiana. (This, by the way, remained in the hospital parking lot for many, many months afterwards. Josephine was right, these probates took a while.) He was never to return to his beloved shop with all the wonderful memories, the antique barber chairs, the tools of his profession, straight razors, combs, the towels draped over the arms of the chairs ready for the next day's customers. It brought tears to my eyes.

There again was mail in between the doors. I thoughtlessly scooped it up and put it in my jacket pocket to look at it later. My mission was to find appropriate clothing for Nelson…a navy suit, white shirt, underwear, one sock and a golf cap. Also some tees, golf balls and his new putter was a must. I wasn't Nancy Lopez, but I loved playing golf and as a golfer I put things in perspective. The sky is blue, the clouds are white and please dear God, let there be greens!

Why couldn't I find a tie? I knew from his driver's license picture that he wore bow ties, but where were they? The thought kept creeping in the back of my mind. Did he really live here? Aha, I found a hanger with about 100 untied ties. Apparently he tied his own…how clever. I chose a red and blue paisley one to match his suit. By the way, the plants had died. Alas!

We headed back to the funeral home to discuss the program. I had Nelson's driver's license with me, it was the only picture I had of him. We chose it for the front of the program and a golfer's prayer on the back.

> *"Lord, when my last putt has dropped into the cup, and the light of my last day has faded, may I be able to turn in to you, a scorecard to show I did my best." Amen.*

The plans were final. Viewing was to be held on Tuesday, February 28, 2006, at 1P.M. to 9P.M. The funeral service would be on Wednesday, March 1, 2006 at 10:00A.M.

-28-

On Tuesday, February 28th at 1P.M. Jim and I walked into the funeral home and were greeted by Nicholas Taylor and his family.

They escorted us to the parlor where Nelson lay in the beautiful Batesville casket that we had chosen. A lovely floor vase of flowers sat to one side with a card, "With deepest sympathy, the Volunteer Advocates for Seniors Program, St. Margaret Mercy Health Care Centers."

This funeral should be personal with family and friends gathering to pay tribute to Nelson's life. Family and friends should be able to remember Nelson, say a prayer and see him for the last time, as they remembered him. But not like this…he was wearing a long tie, it wasn't even his tie. Nelson never wore a long tie, always a bow tie. I didn't want to be picky, especially since the Taylor family had been so accommodating but, where was the bow tie I had brought them for Nelson to wear?

Nicholas explained that no one except his father knew how to tie a bow tie and his father was on vacation in Mexico and not sure when he would return. We would have to find an already tied bow tie. So Jim and Nicholas set out driving down 79th St. in search of a bow tie. They went to the Sears store on 79th St. and numerous other shops. (The same Sears where I learned to drive my Dad's car in that parking lot 50 years ago.)

I stayed alone with Nelson; he looked so peaceful. I placed my hand over his and reflected on the past four months.

It seemed to me that Jim and I knew more about Nelson than anyone. All of his friends or co-workers had a different story to tell, bits and pieces, but no one knew the entire story. I think that was the way Nelson wanted it.

The detective work we performed to uncover his finances (of which I was pretty certain he had lost track of long before the dementia set in), the family search and the support of all Nelson's friends was an incredible journey. I hoped Nelson saw it that way too, but I really doubted it. Nelson was a very private person, his affairs were private, and we had invaded this. I could only hope that he understood, but by golly we needed a bow tie and Jim and Nicholas had returned empty handed.

Many friends visited, friends of 40 to 50 years duration; 79th St. lost a friend. We spent much of the afternoon talking with Mavis Sims, a pretty lady barber who at one time had worked with Nelson. She thought that Nelson's brother, Joseph, may be alive, but no one knew for sure. I thought we probably could have found out had we more time and I hated to think Joseph would miss his brother's funeral. Jim and I left the funeral parlor early to find a bow tie. I hated to ruminate and I didn't want to pray for a bow tie, but thinking back it kept me focused. We had also lost a friend, a very dear friend.

We stopped at many stores on the way back to Indiana but no bow ties.

March 1, 2006 was the day of the funeral which was held at 10:00A.M. in loving memory of Nelson J. Anderson, Jr., mostly known to his friends as "Andy" or "Junior" and to his family as "Uncle Nelson".

Would you believe that Nelson wore his paisley bow tie? Nicholas' father had returned from his vacation late the evening before and tied the bow. As I've said before, "it's the little things".

Jim and I greeted folks as they entered the funeral parlor, introduced ourselves as Nelson's guardians and passed out the programs. The programs were perfect; Joyce was right, everyone wanted one. In fact, Nicholas had to quickly print more. All of Nelson's friends that we had met over the past months were gathered here. Vanessa Nathan and Becky Pryor from VAS Program were there. We shook hands and we hugged. All who stood and lingered at the casket had tears in their eyes; Nelson was loved and respected. Seventy-five people signed the registry and attended the service. My son, Dave, attended and sat with me and Jim. I believe he was concerned and worried about me.

The service was lovely; the scriptures, the prayers, the songs, especially the songs. The first selection, "What a Friend We Have in Jesus" was sung by Mrs. Lester, a fine looking 80 some or more year old little lady with a strong voice. It was followed by "Because He Lives" which rang out through the parlor loud and clear. I heard a few "Amen's" and "Glory-be's" in the audience. Acknowledgments of condolences were spoken by friends who approached the pulpit and shared their memories of Nelson. Love was in the air.

The eulogy by Reverend Nicholas Taylor was everything we could have hoped for; he got to know Nelson too. The final song selection was, "You are so beautiful". It was so appropriate, not a dry eye. The benediction and recessional followed with everyone expressing their final goodbyes past the casket. An announcement was made to join us in repast at the Hard Times Restaurant. I met Ruth Williams, Nelson's sister, and her daughter, Tamara; Michael Anderson and his half brother, Cayler David were there; all so humble, just like Nelson, FAMILY.

In my mind I was thinking, "What a surprise you have waiting for you."

Jim took Michael aside and said, "Get a lawyer, don't wait, do it today."

I waited until everyone had left and stood looking at Nelson for the last time. "You sure look elegant. Rest in peace my friend, rest in peace." I slipped another golf ball in his pocket…you just never know.

-29-

The repast menu consisted of tossed green garden salad, fried and baked chicken with dressing, mashed potatoes, green beans, dinner rolls and cornbread with butter, hot peach cobbler, coffee and tea. It was a very nice buffet and a special thank you to Josephine Wade and her staff for their efficiency and kindness.

Most of the friends and family came to the repast. I had the pleasure of sitting next to Mr. McCoy who you will remember we first met standing in front of the barber shop on 79th St. when we were taking out some of Nelson's belongings including the loose change and the rolled up coins from the drawers next to the barber chairs. He's a perfect game. Mr. McCoy knew from being a regular customer that there was always a lot of change in those drawers. I guess I always felt I needed to explain to him that the money went to the hospital safe in Nelson's account, and now was my chance. He remembered, and said he always wondered what we were doing there. He said he was glad to know that no one else had been able to go into the shop. I felt much better too. Mr. McCoy knew Nelson saved all his change.

I thought, yes, Nelson saved, you have no idea how much Nelson saved.

It was a pleasant luncheon. Everyone seemed to enjoy the meal and the company. Everything was coming to an end, the families were close, the friends were wrapped up with their memories and it was time for closure. Soon Nelson would be on his way via Delta Airlines to Nashville, Tennessee to be buried with his family. We again thanked Nicholas for all he had done for us. He said, “our door is always open.” We laughed and felt grateful for all the friends we had made. Jim had spoken to Michael and now Vanessa from VAS was giving Michael her advice. He would keep in touch. Everyone had closure except me. I had an uneasy, unfinished feeling. Yes, I knew about grieving and I knew the different stages but this was different. I wanted everyone to know Nelson; I don’t think I was ready for closure.

The following days were spent writing “thank you” cards to everyone who attended Nelson’s service and to those who were unable to, but had him in their thoughts and prayers.

Jim and I needed to return to the nursing home. We stopped at a local bakery on 95th St. and picked up two pounds of butter cookies to take with us to the home with our thanks. We had to pick up Nelson's belongings and return them to VAS to be sent to the family. I also had to write our final report to the Superior Court of Lake County. Final, I wasn't ready for final.

The next Sunday in church (we are members of Peace Lutheran Church in Schererville, Indiana), we sang the hymn "Because He Lives". Tears welled up in my eyes, I felt choked, I couldn't sing and I loved this hymn. I poked Jim and said, "Nelson is here." He smiled and gave me that look of "yeah, sure". I looked down, and on the lapel of my coat sat a ladybug. This was March. For sure Nelson was here!

-30-

About two weeks after the funeral I received a call from John Johnson, Nelson's friend. He called to inquire about the disposition of Nelson's barber chairs at the shop. He said a friend of his was interested. I gave him the name of the attorney that was handling Nelson's affairs. We talked a bit about Nelson and he said in closing, "Thank you for doing right by my friend Andy." This meant more to me than I could ever imagine and I thanked him.

One evening getting ready to take the dog for a walk, I reached for my warmest coat and put my hands in my pockets for my gloves. It was bitter cold. I had forgotten…there was the mail from Nelson's shop that I had stuffed into my pocket. One was this letter from Marshall Field's & Co.

Marshall Field's

09/09/05

NELSON J ANDERSON
NELSON J ANDERSON
650 E 79TH ST
CHICAGO IL 60619-3068

1302702

DEAR NELSON J ANDERSON AND NELSON J ANDERSON,

THANK YOU FOR YOUR CREDIT REQUEST. WE REGRET WE ARE UNABLE TO APPROVE IT. WE USED A SCORING SYSTEM WHICH ASSIGNS NUMERICAL VALUES TO INFORMATION WE CONSIDER IN EVALUATING AN APPLICATION. THESE VALUES ARE BASED ON ANALYSIS OF REPAYMENT HISTORIES OF MANY CONSUMERS. AFTER SCORING YOUR APPLICATION, WE WERE UNABLE TO APPROVE YOUR CREDIT REQUEST FOR THE FOLLOWING REASONS:

INSUFFICIENT LENGTH OF CREDIT HISTORY

OUR DECISION WAS BASED IN WHOLE OR IN PART ON DATA FROM THE CONSUMER REPORTING AGENCY SHOWN BELOW.

TRANS UNION CORPORATION
2 BALDWIN PLACE
PO BOX 1000
CHESTER PA 19022
(800) 888-4213

YOU HAVE A RIGHT UNDER THE FAIR CREDIT REPORTING ACT TO KNOW THE INFORMATION IN YOUR CREDIT FILE AT THE CONSUMER REPORTING AGENCY. IF YOU HAVE ANY QUESTIONS CONCERNING YOUR REPORT PLEASE CONTACT THE CONSUMER REPORTING AGENCY LISTED ABOVE. THE AGENCY DID NOT MAKE THE DECISION TO DECLINE YOUR CREDIT REQUEST AND IS UNABLE TO SUPPLY THE SPECIFIC REASON(S) FOR OUR DECISION.

YOU CAN OBTAIN, WITHIN SIXTY (60) DAYS OF RECEIPT OF THIS NOTICE, A FREE COPY OF YOUR REPORT FROM THE CONSUMER REPORTING AGENCY ABOVE. YOU ALSO HAVE THE RIGHT TO CONTACT THE AGENCY TO DISPUTE THE ACCURACY OR COMPLETENESS OF ANY INFORMATION IN THE REPORT.

IF YOU HAVE ANY QUESTIONS ABOUT THIS LETTER, CONTACT US AT
MARSHALL FIELD'S, PO BOX 8103, LORAIN OH 44055, (440) 233-2524, OR YOUR NEAREST STORE.

SINCERELY,

MARSHALL FIELD'S
CREDIT SERVICES

that simply stated Nelson had his credit request denied due to insufficient credit history.

I couldn't believe it. Here was Marshall Field's & Co. denying Nelson a credit card. Didn't they know he always paid his bills on time and would never cheat anyone? Apparently not! Didn't they know he was an honest man who did an honest day's work? Apparently not! How could they have turned him down? Didn't they know he was from 79th Street? Didn't they know he was a millionaire…a multi-millionaire and still counting?

Apparently not…we did!

Some weeks later St. Margaret Mercy Hospital forwarded a letter addressed to Jim and me. It was this letter from his brother, Joseph.

I felt sad. I was glad Joseph was alive, but sad that he had missed seeing his brother before he died and was not able to attend the funeral. Maybe we didn't try hard enough to find him or

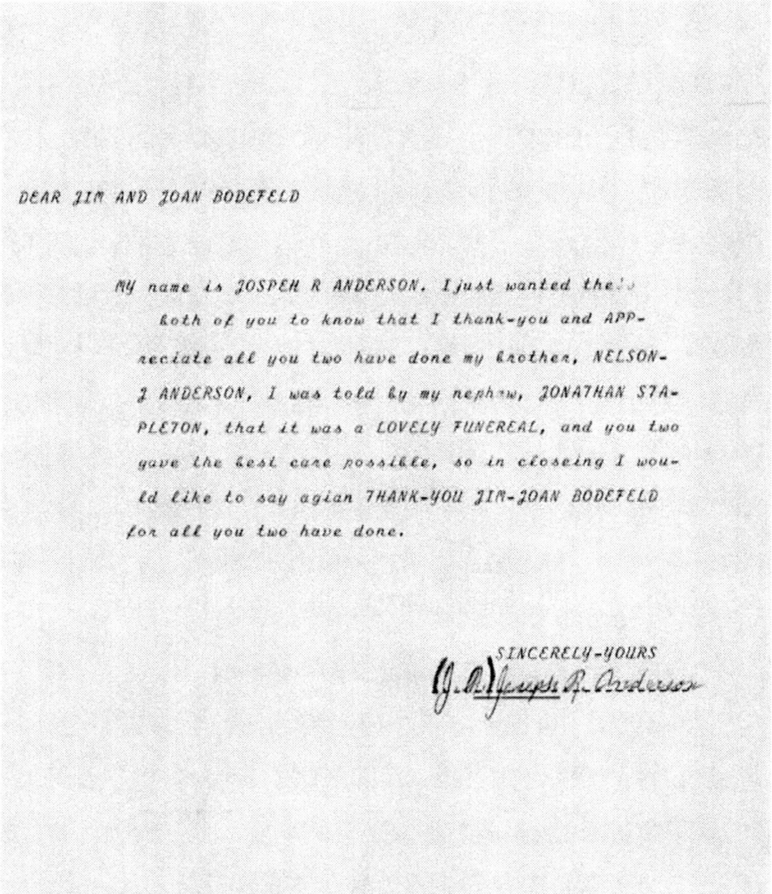

DEAR JIM AND JOAN BODEFELD

MY name is JOSPEH R ANDERSON. I just wanted the both of you to know that I thank-you and APP-reciate all you two have done my brother, NELSON-J ANDERSON, I was told by my nephew, JONATHAN STA-PLETON, that it was a LOVELY FUNEREAL, and you two gave the best care possible, so in closeing I wou-ld like to say agian THANK-YOU JIM-JOAN BODEFELD for all you two have done.

SINCERELY-YOURS

(J. R.) Joseph R. Anderson

Nelson's Brother's letter

maybe he just didn't want to be found. It was all too much; I couldn't look back.

Life goes on, well…sometimes it pauses…or as Nelson would have said "a little of this and a little of that and a little something in between."

Spring was here. I belong to two ladies golf leagues, one at Lincoln Oaks in Crete, Illinois (the same one where Nelson and his friends played golf) and Scherwood Club in Schererville, Indiana. Life is good, I loved my job, my family, my nine grandchildren and Jim and I were still active with the VAS Program. So what was wrong? There was a nagging voice in my head…tell about Nelson… write about him.

Jerry Wolfe had moved back to Chicago. We lunched and we talked on the phone often. Nelson was in her thoughts too. I talked to her about my idea of a book. She was a little reluctant, and I respected that. Her memories were dear and belonged to her.

On Christmas Eve 2006 Jim and I received a phone call from Richard Douglas saying "Merry Christmas" and he thanked us again and told us he thinks of us often and we are on his Christmas card list. Imagine that, he remembered us. I felt good. We would never forget Nelson or any of his friends and family but were reluctant to keep in touch. Our job was finished, or was it?

On Christmas Eve 2007 there was a phone call from Melvin Bryant, another of Nelson's friends. He said, "I've been thinking of you and Jim and want to wish you both a Merry Christmas and a Happy New Year." I was thrilled! How special was that? Almost two years had passed and

Melvin Bryant took time out on Christmas Eve to wish us a happy holiday. He not only was thinking of Jim and me, but also of his good friend "Andy". Yes, it will be a good year. I'm going to write a book about yours and my friend "Andy". Yes indeed, it will be a good year!

"Our lives begin to end the day we become silent about things that matter."

This was a quote from Martin Luther King, Jr., U.S. black civil rights leader and clergyman (1929-1968).

Friends & Family

Michael Anderson

We had a quiet breakfast with Michael at Howie's on 14th and Wabash in Chicago on a very cold morning in January 2008. He is a tall, well built man in his 50's, salt and pepper hair, with kind eyes. He lives alone in an apartment close by. He gave me a warm hug and Jim a firm handshake. I sensed he was a little uncomfortable at first telling us he wasn't sure how much help he could be because he hadn't really met his father until he was about 12 years old, the same with his Uncle Nelson.

"My first real memory of my father was looking through the bars of my crib as a baby, maybe about three years old, watching my father chase my mother around the house with a mouse.

I can remember laughing." He became more relaxed, we laughed and he continued.

"They were divorced; my father was a barber and lived above the barber shop on 95th St. I lived with my mother on S. Princeton. I didn't see much of him until one day I was riding my bike with my cousin and he asked me if I wanted to see my father. Sure I did. I was 12. He told me he had some issues with my mother and stepfather; you know how that goes.

"One time my father took me for a ride. We went to Detroit to visit an Aunt Tillie on my Mother's side. She was a caterer and I loved her biscuits. He never would talk much about anything, kind of secretive, I was just glad to be with him. Secrets ran in the family. Uncle Nelson was the same way."

As I sat watching and listening to Michael relay and remember a youthful story, I was saddened. I thought what a kind and sensitive man. I imagined this was what Nelson was like. Michael takes after Nelson, quiet, reserved, with a gentle way about him. I'm sure Nelson was happy he was his nephew. Michael is the Executor of his Uncle Nelson's estate and is overwhelmed with the responsibility but is doing a fine job working with his attorney.

"I think the money came from my Grandmother Ruth's side of the family. I know my father and Uncle Nelson went to Nashville about her estate. There was another brother Joseph, he's kind of a street person, but he shared. My father and uncle saw to that.

"When my father died in 1998, my half sister Sharon didn't have the money to come to Chicago for the funeral, so Uncle Nelson sent her a train ticket, not an airline ticket but a train ticket. He was frugal, but I remember him telling us not to worry, you'll be taken care of, certainly not by our father since he was an alcoholic; we never saw a penny. Uncle Nelson bought the barber shop on 95th St. and it is still there doing business. We hope to sell it.

"I would go to the 79th St. barber shop after my father died and Uncle Nelson would cut my hair. I liked being there; it was like being with my father. He would always give me $20 whether I needed it or not. Sometimes he would have me wait for him to finish with other customers and take me to eat at his favorite soul food restaurant down the street. I liked that. Uncle Nelson took the barber shop over after his Uncle Prince died. We don't think he lived in the back of the shop; he couldn't have slept in that bed…too much stuff on it. A lot of the stuff was his Uncle Prince's. Yes, he saved everything, didn't he? I'm like that too. Maybe he had a room somewhere. No, you're right, we never received any rent bills or saw any rent receipts, and he would have saved them. Strange that he never had a Will. I know it was God's blessing that Uncle Nelson fell out in Indiana." We thought so too; truly a divine intervention.

Richard White and Michael Anderson

Sharon Osborn

"It was a blessing. As a little girl growing up I called him "Uncle Junior". It wasn't a surprise, just a blessing." This was in response to my phone call to Sharon Osborn, Nelson Anderson's niece who lives in Maryland regarding her inheritance.

"I understand you want to write about my family. I am Charles's daughter, although I didn't live with my father. I remember a lot of uncles, George, Ed, Toussaint, and Prince. Uncle Junior lived with Uncle Prince in Chicago. I know my grandmother, Ruth Virginia McKissack, died in childbirth with Nelson's brother Joseph, when they lived in Virginia. My grandfather was the first black dentist in Appalachia Wise, Virginia and they lived above the office. And then he died. I know Uncle Junior lived with his aunts in Nashville; Martha Brown,

Jennie, and his grandmothers, Lutie and Tina. There is a library named for Aunt Martha in Nashville at the Tennessee University, The Martha Brown Library. She was a teacher."

Sharon continued saying, "The family had a lot of property in Nashville. They were an influential family with a lot of land." I could hear the pride in her voice for her heritage, and what a heritage it was.

"When I was about 10 years old I remember traveling with the family to Detroit since we had family there. Uncle Junior always had cool cars. In the 70's he had a Saab which was nice. He also used to like Volkswagens. No, I didn't know where he lived in Chicago. I know I would go to the barber shop to get my hair cut. I guess he had a place. He was a little mysterious; he had a mystique about him. You would have to pick and pull information from him. No, I didn't know Michael then, I met Michael when my father Charles died."

The phone conversation went very well. Sharon is a very pleasant speaking lady who sounded sincere about talking to me about her family. She said she called Nelson every Saturday at the barber shop and they would talk.

"He would tell me he was busy cutting hair and that he would call me back, and he never did. He was a very private man with a private life. I don't know what that man did; he never said. If I needed a dollar he'd give me or my kid's money but you'd have to pay him back. A loan…he said it built character and stability…he was frugal."

I thanked her for her time and information and wished her well.

Bernice Gibson

You know how sometimes when you meet someone or talk to them on the phone it's like you've known them a long time? Well that's what it was like talking to Bernice, Nelson's first cousin. Bernice Gibson lives in Highland Park, Michigan. She's a retired nurse who is also a diabetic and had a leg amputated. Bernice was casual about her disease and said she did very well during her rehabilitation. Diabetes runs in her family.

Bernice is of the McKissack Family, her father was Toussaint (I've also seen it spelled Tucson), Nelson's uncle, brother to Ruth, Nelson's mother. Ruth died in childbirth with Joseph. Bernice said, "You know, back then there was segregation. I remember my grandmother telling me that Ruth was so white she could sit in the front of the bus. Yes, she was very fair."

As I said, I felt comfortable talking with her and I could tell she felt the same way.

"Oh, you're bringing up things I haven't thought about in a long time. You know, we all lived with our Grandmother Tina at various times. I was younger, but I do remember Nelson being there too, before he moved to Iowa with his aunts.

"I always kept in touch with Nelson. He lived with our Uncle Prince in Chicago. No, I'm not sure where. I do remember coming to Chicago with my grandmother to see him. We would go to the show and to dinner; Nelson liked to eat. Sometimes he would come to Detroit to see my father and once Joseph, Nelson's brother came to stay with me for three to four weeks. One morning he woke up and told me he was going to the store to get some writing paper and I never saw him again. That was about 35 years ago. Once about 20 to 25 years ago, Nelson called me and asked a lot of questions…my birth date and social security number. I asked him why and he said he was taking care of business. I didn't think anything of it. He was a businessman. I always assumed he had everything in order, but no idea to this extent. He was always so pleasant, but one time just in conversation he said, 'All people want is my money.' He said he had a Will and everyone would be taken care of.

"I know the grandparents had a lot of property in Nashville and sold some, and I knew Nelson had stock." (This was a very notable family going back many generations.) I told Bernice I had done some genealogy work and would send her my findings.

"Nelson and I talked quite often on the phone. The last time I saw Nelson I visited with him in Chicago. He came to Thomas' house, my nephew. No, other times if I visited I would see him at the barber shop, only in the front; I never went into the back. I thought he lived there. Every year I would get a Christmas card from him and the address was the shop. He always remembered. But Christmas of '06 I didn't get one so I asked my nephew, Thomas Banks, to go by the barber shop and see if everything was all right. That's how I found out about you."

I thanked Bernice for her information and as Bernice said, I had brought back a lot of memories. Sounded like good ones.

That was in February. I had occasion to call Bernice again six months later and we discussed my book. It was then she casually mentioned that her husband had also written a book, “Ode to Life”.

I said, “Bernice, you never told me that before.”

She laughed and went on to say that her husband Robert had been dead about 20 years.

“Oh my, it doesn’t seem that long ago.” She was quiet for a moment and so was I. “Yes” she went on, “He performed under the name Gip Roberts, as an Emcee, comedian, singer and dancer. He played all the clubs; that was the entertainment era. He played with all the big names, Red Foxx, B.B King, Gladys Knight, Louis Armstrong, all the people from Motown in Detroit. The building still stands on West Grand Ave. today. He played in Chicago at the High Chaparral, the Club De Lisa, Robert’s Lounge in a hotel but I can’t remember which one. We would all go to see him, yes Nelson too, all the time.

I was able to travel with him and meet so many of the stars. He played at the Apollo in New York City also.

"Remember Thomas Banks, you met him at the repast for Nelson? He's my husband's nephew."

"Yes, I remember Tom. He was at the table with Vanessa and kept her entertained." That was exciting! More good memories! Thanks Bernice.

William Blair

"He had a great smile, always joking and laughing. That was Nelson." That was William Blair's comment when I spoke to him on the phone prior to meeting for breakfast a few days later. Mr. Blair did go to St. Margaret Mercy Hospital after speaking to the St. John police officer. He brought a friend, Irma, with him.

They both thought that Nelson knew them but, "Maybe not for sure, because he always had a great smile for everyone and he was kind of acting natural. He did tell me when I asked him what he was doing out there, he told me he thought he was at the golf course and that he thought I was coming to get him, to take him home. Where would I have taken him? Good question, I never knew where he lived. No, he didn't push it to take him out, just told me next time I came to see him I could take him. I came to see him a few times after that while he was still in the hospital. He had a way of making you think he was okay, but he wasn't. He was confused."

William Blair and Irma Adams

We had breakfast at the Starlight on 83rd and Kedzie Ave. in Chicago where Jim and I met William Blair and his friend, Irma Adams. Irma is a petite, very attractive senior lady who bragged as she did a little dance. "Yes, I'm 83 and love to dance. I know all the senior centers and go to them often. I've lived in Englewood for the past 60 years, and my daughter lives nearby.

"I worked at the Post Office, sat side by side with Nelson for 20 years. He never missed a day.

"One day he came to work and said he was leaving and he did; I guessed he retired. That was in the 80's and I never knew him very well, nobody did. I was from Iowa and so was he. That's all I knew. He had a barber shop, his other job, and one time I asked him, 'Why don't you hire another barber?' He said, 'If I hired someone I'd have to watch them; they might run off with something.'

"He liked to work alone. I was so surprised when I saw him in the hospital and he was almost bald. He always had beautiful silky straight hair and always dressed so nice. Of course, I saw him in a winter coat, a long dressy one with a scarf. Why would you ask that?" (She asked in response to my question regarding his belongings). Then she asked me. "Why are you doing this anyway?"

I had to laugh to myself, why? Good question. But someone had to tell his story, and no one knew him as well as Jim and me. No one!

Mr. Blair was a good faithful friend to Nelson, also a senior, with a very active lifestyle. He was a grey haired, balding, nice looking gentleman with sparkling eyes that twinkle when speaking, and always a smile. He was born into a large family in Ohio. He came to Chicago when he was 18.

"Too many rules at home, I volunteered for the Army but they put me in the Navy. How's that! My Mama sure didn't like me joining the service. I spent time at Great Lakes in 1943 and by the time I was 20, I felt like I was 20,000 miles away from home.

"I spent time in Taiwan, Okinawa, Tokyo and the Philippines. I loved the Navy, but I returned to Chicago after my tour and I worked in a factory. I went to a couple of trade schools and got a couple of diplomas. I was still in my early 20's. I sold insurance, got married and eventually got a job with the Post Office and worked there for 40 years. I also was a Timekeeper like Nelson, worked right beside him.

"Nelson liked to go places and had a lot of interests, always laughing, but he was secretive. He would drive all over the United States by himself. He wasn't friendly about traveling with anyone; he was a loner. He drove a Volkswagen and went all over, to California, Florida, Carolinas, Detroit, Iowa. He liked to drive. Yes, talked a lot but never much about him. I always thought he was from Iowa and moved to Nashville. I think he was raised by his aunts, but you tell me it was the other way around. He was born in Nashville and raised in Iowa.

"After he retired I didn't see much of him. I always knew he had another job and that he was a barber, so one day I called him and got a haircut. After that I went to see him once a month. If I got to the barber shop before he opened, I'd wait and here he would come from down the street. I guess I thought he lived nearby. Sometimes we'd go down the street to his favorite restaurant for soul food. Yes, as I said, he was always smiling, but he talked around everything. When you would ask him a question that he didn't want to answer, he would just smile."

Both Mr. Blair and Irma were relaxed while talking with Jim and me about their friend and about their own

lives which we appreciated. Mr. Blair told us he lived on S. Elizabeth St. with his wife and that his granddaughter lived with them. He is a group leader for the "Glamour" Travel Club for seniors. They travel around the USA in motor coaches. He smiled broadly while he told us about all the fun they have. He also is president of the St. Joachim Parish "Happy Action Seniors Club". In October '07 he received a State of Illinois Crime Prevention Award as a volunteer; he was recommended by the 6th District police commander and was so proud. Along with all his activities, he still makes time to take his family or friends to their doctor appointments whenever he is asked. We could all use a good friend like Mr. Blair.

Joyce Franklin

"Bless his heart, he was such a gentleman, just write about him." Beautiful words from a beautiful woman. This sweet phrase was spoken by Joyce Franklin, an energetic and lively lady. Jim and I met Joyce for breakfast at Army and Lou's Restaurant, 422 E. 75th St. Army and Lou's is one of the oldest black-owned restaurants in the Midwest. Since 1945 this award winning restaurant is noted for serving high end soul food and was a favorite dining spot for Harold Washington, Chicago's first black mayor. According to a web source, Army was a political reporter for the Defender and Lou was his wife. There are different owners at this time. Joyce remembered the restaurant being on 39th St. at one time.

The walls were all covered with beautiful large paintings, mostly of women holding babies or very young children. The waitress explained it was for the upcoming Mother's Day buffet. Our breakfast was excellent. The atmosphere was like a wonderful piece of history.

Joyce is the owner and operator of Joyce's "As You Like It" Barber Shop, 624 East 79th St., one block from Nelson's shop. She is a graduate of Eulien Barber School and over the years has had some very influential customers, such as Congressman Harold Washington, prior to his becoming Mayor. Also, former Chicago Police Superintendant Rice and many, many more not so influential but much loved and appreciated. Her shop is filled with posters, autographed photos and memorabilia of sports figures (Jim drooled over those). Joyce worked at the shop in 1975 and took it over in 1977. She said that Nelson was very helpful during that transitional period.

Joyce called Nelson 'Mr. Anderson' and said most folks called him Jr. Nelson also was a friend of Joyce's father-in-law, Willie Franklin,

Sr., a barber at 517 E.79th St. at that time.

"They had the greatest respect for each other. Nelson and I were not competitive. I could always count on him if I ran out of something since he had everything and was always so organized. He was a professional all the way." Joyce became a little teary at this point in our conversation. We paused, and quietly reflected on the day she and I and Jim opened the door in the back of Nelson's shop. Joyce also expressed her feelings of how different his shop was compared to his living space.

"Oh, I knew he lived back there. I should have watched him closer. I should have gotten emergency numbers."

"No Joyce, I doubted he would have given you anything." Joyce was another good friend who cared deeply about others.

Joyce knew a lot of Nelson's customers. He had also cut her hair. "He was slow, he took his time, and he never charged me. I'd try to pay him but it wasn't the money, he just loved doing it; a lot of people he wouldn't charge. Sometimes I'd say, 'Hurry up, I've got customers too'. It didn't matter. It was a love fest with all his customers. His shop was standard, nothing updated, but his customers loved it. He had a towel service and his uniforms were always clean and starched. And he saved everything. I remember someone would want to know when a friend had passed and he'd go in the back and bring out the obituary. He knew where everything was. When he got ready to do something, he'd do it.

"He always ate three meals a day, never snacked, he'd close up and go eat or go on vacation, just like that. He'd say "be back in a week." He loved to play golf. No, I didn't know he was a diabetic until we saw the insulin in the refrigerator, remember? No, I didn't know he had a shop on 95th St. either. You're right; he wouldn't have given me any numbers."

Joyce Franklin

Every Monday on Joyce's day off she would drive to the nursing home in

Oak Lawn to visit and to shave Nelson. She said, "I would ask him, 'who am I?' He would answer, 'Joyce Franklin,' and he would smile broadly and say, 'from 79th St.' He knew me, I'd tell him, 'all your customers miss you,' and he'd say, "We'll meet again. Tell them I'll see them." I knew what he meant, if we all could have that." Joyce continued these weekly visits until he died. She was the first call I made.

Louise Williams

"Back on the 9", Friday, April 12, 2008. A single page flyer advertised "Wezee's Soul Food" Restaurant, 616 E. 79th St. After opening in 1999 and then being closed for two years, Louise Williams is glad to be back on 79th St. "This is where it's at, 79th St., this is the heart of the city." Louise, known as "Wezee" is owner, chief cook and bottle washer of the newly reopened restaurant which was two blocks from Nelson's barber shop. Wezee is a very attractive lady with a beautiful smile. For the past two years she had owned and operated a restaurant on 23rd and Michigan called "Memories". She said it was a great place for a soul food eatery. There weren't any like it in that area and business was good except for parking, a major problem due to a lot of construction going on in that area. "My church is at 16th and Wabash, good property down there, but I'm glad to be back on the 9."

The wall behind and to the side of the counter was adorned with a life size photo of Harold Washington, who she spoke of with reverence. The breakfast was Jim's second soul food adventure in a week and he was not complaining; the food was good. Wezee warmly welcomed us and talked openly of her favorite customer Junior, as she called Nelson.

"I knew he was Mr. Anderson, but we all called him Junior. He was quiet, came in every day with his newspaper for breakfast…oatmeal, wheat toast and coffee, no sugar." I asked if she knew he was diabetic.

Louise Willi

"No, he never said anything about that, he never complained about anything, always patient, no matter how busy we were, he was a gentleman. He was well educated, very polite and professional. He was orderly, always clean and fresh. And no matter the weather, he always wore a little jacket and a cap, a golf cap. No, I never saw him with a scarf or boots, or winter coat, just a light jacket. I knew he stayed behind the barber shop. We had both rented the garages behind the shop, so I'd see him there."

She went on to say, "He would tell me sometimes he was driving to Indiana to visit his sister. No, I never noticed any confusion and he came here for lunch too. He'd bring his friends with him, his golfing buddies. I knew it took him a long time to cut hair; he talked all the time. He cut hair by appointment only.

"I went to the funeral and I thought, who put this altogether? It was nice." We thanked her and wished her success on the 9.

Richard Douglas

"I've always said you have an open invitation anytime. We all called him Andy." February 28, 2008, a very cold and snowy morning, Jim and I met and had breakfast at the Country Kitchen on 87th and Cottage Grove in Chicago with a group of Nelson's friends, mostly retirees from the Post Office. "Chicago Postal Golfers Club Inc." Richard Douglas has kept in touch with Jim and me these past years. What a delightful gentleman! All of Nelson's friends are delightful gentlemen, fun loving and easy talking, laughing, smiling and all talking at the same time.

Mr. Douglas seemed to be in charge and said he did the mailings for the club. He remembered asking Nelson a long time ago what address he should use for the golf outing mailings, and Nelson said to just use the P.O. Box number in Chicago which he did.

"I never could understand why he kept it all those years even after he retired." Richard Douglas was born and raised in Chicago, "from 35th St.", now living with his family on S. Michigan Ave. He had just returned from California, where he had visited with his granddaughter's family and his new great-granddaughter. He brought pictures and passed them around.

Now these fellows have been together probably over 40 years, maybe longer. That started a very long cross talking discussion and truthfully I got lost. It began as a bowling league starting out on 115th and Halsted Streets in Chicago and then began their golfing outings with breakfast here at the Country Kitchen maybe since the 70's.

"We get here about 10:00 and stay till they throw us out around 2P.M." Apparently this restaurant is a great meeting place with good accommodations for getting together because "Campbell Soup" fellows were also there having fun.

"I've known Andy more than 30 or 40 years. I knew him quite well personally but he never confided in me or anyone else I knew. I didn't know about the barber shop on 95th St. or even that he had brothers. We've had our golf outings traveling across the states; I believe I was in the military service when I started playing. We'd take bus trips to San Antonio, Biloxi, Pensacola, Mobile, and Myrtle Beach. Andy would always know where we were going, but he never went with us. We'd be out on the course and turn around and there he was on the hole behind us. He just took two clubs, a five iron and a putter. One time in Biloxi, we were talking about golf and he said, "I'm leaving and going to South Carolina." I asked him if he had relatives there and he said, "I've got some friends there." There were just tidbits, South Carolina, Nashville. He never would say or go into detail, just conversation. We didn't think anything of it.

"Andy always cut my hair. If you happened to get in around meal time he'd close up shop and you'd go eat with him. I think that was the way with everyone. He never had a fee, somewhere between $3 and $7, and I know the union price was at least $16; most of us were postal workers. The last time I was in the barber shop was about a month before he got sick. He seemed fine, never had any idea. No, he wasn't confused. I think he had a mini stroke."

God bless you Richard Douglas, you were a good friend to the end. What more could anyone ask for?

Richard Douglas

Bob Seymour

"The best kept secret in South Chicago Land," Lincoln Oaks Golf Course, 395 E. Richton Rd., Crete, Illinois.

So reads the business card of Bob Seymour, General Manager of Lincoln Oaks Golf Course. During breakfast with the postal boys it seemed golf was synonymous with Lincoln Oaks Golf Course. They all had at one time or another (and some still) played in a golf league there and just the mention of Bob's name brought about more cross talk between the fellows. They all laughed and remembered what fun they had and how accommodating Bob was.

"He always took good care of us no matter how crowded it was on the course, really nice guy." They all agreed. I did too. This time I could join in on the conversation.

"Oh, you know Bob too," asked Mr. Douglas? "Sure I do, he does the same for the ladies."

Bob remembers the fellows from the postal league as "fun loving gentlemen, always a pleasure, always laughing and joking, a lot of fun."

Lincoln Oaks was my course too. Every Tuesday morning, "The Tuesday

Tee-Offers," were 29 of the best women golfers. Oh, that sounds like I'm bragging, well, fun loving anyway. I wonder what he says about the ladies. I'm just kidding Bob.

Huey Scott

Seems everyone was surprised when Huey told the story of Nelson and him driving together to Biloxi,

Mississippi in Nelson's Volkswagen Beetle. They stopped in Nashville to see Nelson's family, stayed for a while, visited and continued on their way. "I think it might have been his aunt or his grandmother."

Huey Scott was born in Fordyce, Arkansas. He very proudly stated, "I'm 88." Huey's friends also proudly chimed in that Huey was an aviation engineer in the Army in 1942, and helped build the airstrip at Eglin Air Force Base in Florida.

"I came to Chicago in 1947 and worked at the main Post Office with Andy. I retired in 1983. You know, when Andy and I drove to Biloxi to play golf, he had to stay with us because he had to bring me back home. I thought he lived behind the barber shop too but he never invited me back there. He kept his car behind the shop." I asked Huey if Nelson had ever talked to him or any of the others about his cousin, Doc Cheatham. That name brought a roar and a lot of cross talk among the boys. They all knew of Doc Cheatham, the trumpet player, who played with Louis Armstrong in the 20's. They had either seen him or heard him play and all were a little in awe that this man was Andy's cousin.

I knew he was Nelson's cousin, I had seen the wonderful smiling eyes when Nelson and I would reminisce.

Milton Williams

Milton was born in Little Rock, Arkansas and came to Chicago in 1948. Milton was Nelson's supervisor at the Post Office. "Andy was a Timekeeper and very good at it. He was kind of mysterious, I never heard him say a bad thing about anyone. He was kind of different, but you accepted him, and loved him. He was a good listener and loved golf. He always stayed in touch with the group. He always came late and played by himself; he would just appear. I sometimes had access to passes for the major golf events and I would always give them to Andy. He met many players and caddies. They would even come to the barber shop on 79th St. and sign autographs. The last time I was in his shop, he showed me a new putter and insisted we practice with it. Andy was coy and smart. He may have been sliding a bit and I think to keep from embarrassing himself, he gave me some general answers that would cover everything. No, I don't think I worried about him at that time."

Mr. Williams retired from the Post Office in 1986, and is active with the Tuskegee Airmen. He himself was a WWII pilot, a lieutenant in the Air Force.

"I knew at an early age that I wanted to be a pilot. We lived near an airfield in Little Rock and I used to sneak off and hang around with the white pilots. In high school I joined a group to build model airplanes. Yes, I always wanted to be a pilot. I went to Falander Smith College, and then volunteered for the Air Force. I thanked him also for his service to our country. These men were loyal.

Clifton Martin

Another good friend was Clifton Martin. He was born in Detroit, Michigan, and moved to Chicago when only one year old. He proudly showed me a fine leather triple fold case displaying his retired police badge. Clifton is a retired Chicago Police Sergeant. He retired after serving 34 years on the Force. His last assignment was the 7th District, Englewood. "I knew Andy from going to the barber shop. Andy was a 79th St. Institution. He never said much about himself but he was a good listener especially when you talked about investments; that would really peak his interest. Some of the fellows here are with the Tuskegee Airmen, fighter pilots from WWII, a black service unit. Let me introduce you to Moses Jones."

Moses Jones

"I've been part of this group for two or three years and I really didn't know that man, but have you heard of the Tuskegee Airmen, the black pilots of World War II?" I couldn't say that I did remember that.

"Well of course not, they didn't want you to," he said. (I didn't ask who 'they' were, not today.)

This was my introduction to Moses Jones. He was born and raised in Chicago, and was a retired Math teacher from South Shore High School. Prior to that, he was a teacher at the Educational Vocational Guidance Center on the west side of Chicago. Moses presently is tutoring young folks at the Blackstone Library. He proudly presented this card to me and promptly

TUSKEGEE AIRMEN, INC.
Chicago DODO Chapter

YOUNG EAGLES
FREE INTRODUCTORY FLIGHTS
AT GARY/CHICAGO AIRPORT

AGES 7-17

In Chicago Call: (312) 409-5621
In Gary Call: (888) 235-9824
www.taichicago.org

began showing the group a film on his laptop. Sitting next to me was Milton

Williams also of the Tuskegee Airmen, who also had a computer program that his daughter had taken of the 'Young Eagles' at the Gary Airport. This program, he explained, was nationwide and for youngsters from ages 7 through 17, each second Saturday of the month, to enjoy and be educated in aviation. Each child would be taken up in an airplane either singularly or in a group for the experience and joy of flying. We all watched and I was certainly educated, right there on the spot. Hey, I was here to get information, I soaked it up. I thanked everyone and promised to educate myself and look further on the internet, which I did.

The Tuskegee Airmen, originally 332nd Fighter Group, were a group of 450 fighter pilots trained at the Tuskegee Institute in Alabama. They were the first African Americans to be trained as WWII military pilots in the

U.S. Army Air Corps. The Tuskegee Airmen challenged America's racist attitudes with the willingness to give their lives to their country. They were still segregated and the tails of their aircraft were painted red. They were known as the "red tails". But later they

(Standing) Moses Jones
(Seated L to R) Russell London, Milton Williams, Clifton Martin

were known as the "red tail angels" because their performance became legendary. They were the most "requested" fighter escorts by the white bomber pilots. Of the group 66 gave their lives in combat and 32 were captured as prisoners of war. Thank you Moses for my homework assignment that I won't ever forget.

Today the Chicago Chapter establishes Educational Assistance Programs to grant financial awards to students who demonstrate the qualities of the Tuskegee Airmen: Vision, Commitment, Thirst, Honor, Integrity and Respect.

Russell London

"I wouldn't be where I am today if it weren't for my wife, Alberta. She's a retired school teacher who made me what I am." This was happily spoken by Russell London. Russell was born in New York and raised in Chicago. "I worked at the Post Office with the group at one time, but most of them know me from the bowling alley going back to the 60's. I started golfing with the group, the first time going to Biloxi in 1979 on a bus trip. We took bus trips to San Antonio, Myrtle Beach, wherever there was a golf course.

"I don't remember Nelson very well because he never went on the bus with us, but he always showed up. Yes, we had some fun times. In the 60's after the Post Office, I worked for UPS, then for Lorillard Co. selling tobacco products and Hiram Walker Co. I finally retired after 26 years with Judge & Dolph, a liquor distribution company in Chicago. As I said, I attribute Alberta; she made me."

That was very nice. Even nicer for me, I'll see Russell once in a while; we both golf at Lincoln Oaks in Crete. I may run into a few more of you guys on the links, FORE!

John Turner

"I was kind of upset to have you take care of Andy. I thought 'Why them?' You can't blame me for thinking that." This was from John

Turner, the very honest John Turner. I was taken back a little. We had never sensed that feeling from any of Nelson's friends at that time; in fact

Jim and I always felt and were surprised that we had been accepted from the start. John assured me that the feeling didn't last long and I told him that we felt comfortable with all of Nelson's friends in doing our job as guardians. Well, well, that was a surprise. Continuing on, I left John to interview last because he sat very quiet with a sweet smile and seemed kind of shy so I wanted to talk to him alone, and I got the honesty which I appreciated.

John went on to tell me he was originally from Alabama, but had come to Chicago in 1947. He also worked at the Post Office with Nelson in the same department and like the others, Nelson cut his hair. "I was bald but I went anyway and he just trimmed around. I never knew he had another shop on 95th St. He was secretive about himself. Oh yes, we talked a lot about sports and cars. I bought a Volkswagen because he had one and he talked good about it. He always wanted to go eat, you had to go with him or wait until he came back. At one time he told me where he lived. I can't remember but it wasn't behind the barber shop. Remember I met you at the hospital, I'm sure he knew me; he said I had two girls but I really have two boys. Sure we talked, a lot, I don't know, just about everything."

I thanked John for his honesty and now it was about time for all of us to be kicked out. Not really, but I was exhausted.

Mavis Sims

"I worked in the shop from 1971 until 1984. I'm a barber! I still barber at my home; I can pick and choose, but I like to play cards too." This was a delightful conversation with Mavis

Sims talking with me about Nelson and her years working with him. Mavis sounded a little guarded at first but I reminded her of all the memories she shared with me at the funeral and we chatted more comfortably. Mavis is an attractive lady, very statuesque and I bet she was quite an asset in the barber shop.

"A lot of my customers worked at the Post Office, no, I haven't seen any of his old customers. We also had two more barbers at the shop, Mr. Brown and Gene Lawson and there was Lonnie who shined shoes. Mr. Anderson was very private, he didn't do much talking. If he did it was about golf. He loved golf, he got a lot of phone calls at the shop, people calling about his property, but he never talked about it. He had an uncle in Detroit, an uncle in Tennessee and an aunt in Des

Moines; they all left him money after they died."

We talked about Joseph. I told Mavis he was still alive and she said, "Joseph was smart, he had many degrees, don't let anyone tell you he had mental problems. When he came to the barber shop, Mr. Anderson would give him some money, take him out to eat and you wouldn't see him for a while."

Mavis still referred to Nelson as Mr. Anderson. That was nice. She went on to tell me that "he worked in the barber shop from 9A.M. to 2P.M. and then went to work at the Post Office working the 3 to 11 shift. I would close up later in the day." I said to Mavis that Nelson must have trusted her and that kind of surprised me. She said, "I guess he trusted me just so far."

I asked Mavis where Nelson lived and she said, "He lived in back of the shop. At one time he lived with a family on 86th and Prairie and then when his Uncle Prince died he moved into the shop. I know for sure he lived there. Every morning he would leave out the back door to the alley, walk around the block, and come in the front door, just like he was going to work." She didn't seem to think that was odd saying "he was proud to go to work." I hoped we would talk again sometime.

Reverend Nicholas Taylor

"Rest your coat" said Reverend Nicholas Taylor. "Excuse me?" I said. "Rest your coat", he said. I had never heard that expression before. I took off my coat. Jim and I were at the Taylor Funeral Home. "How long has it been?" he asked. Two years I said. The Reverend warmly hugged me and Jim; it was good to see him too.

Nicholas had been so helpful with Nelson's funeral arrangements and service. My first question to him was, "What did you first think when we came to see you about pre-planning a funeral? I remember we showed you our court papers and explained our guardianship role but we were from Indiana, you didn't know us or even Nelson, and you were so kind."

Nicholas said, "I operate that way, I'm here to render service, I'll help in any way I can. And as I remember, you didn't know him either. (We laughed at that one.) After hearing your story about him, I thought it was a blessing to meet people who care this much about another human being. And his mind being the way it was, it's a different world out there. The way he was found, it's like you were his angels sent to him, I truly believe that. If you hadn't come along what would have happened to him? It tells me there is a God. You were his angels like the 23rd Psalm and the Lord's Prayer, 'Evil could have come across him.' What we do here is for the survivors, we honor that person's life. What an interesting journey that you people took upon yourselves."

Nicholas Taylor

Listening to Nicholas I felt like I was in church and we appreciated the kind words. We thanked him again for all his help and guidance with the planning. He said, "I felt obligated to help you, you made up your minds you were not doing anything cheesy." We laughed and reminisced about the way he and Jim had driven up and down 79th St. looking for a pre-tied bow tie, and again how grateful we were to Nicholas for all the extras he did for us and especially for Nelson. No, nothing cheesy for our Nelson.

Tyrone Jordan

"The cream always rises to the top. That's what he would tell me, he always praised me in everything I did. I think I may have been his last customer that Friday night. Well, he was slow barbering, in fact, I dozed in the chair, the kids were playing on the floor, and he seemed okay. It was late and he told my son Tyrell to lock the door. He loved my kids, and I was a die hard for Mr. Anderson.

"He was always nurturing me, encouraging me in everything I did; he was kind of like a counselor or a psychologist, always full of wisdom and telling me to take care of my family."

This was the beginning of our conversation with Sgt. Tyrone Jordan of the Chicago Police Department at his home on 81st and Champlain Ave. This was around the corner from where I grew up. I looked out his kitchen window and could see the back of the house that was my world 60 some years ago. The emotions for me were a bit overwhelming. My Mom and Dad, I could picture the rooms in my house, my piano, the sidewalk where I learned to ride my bike, the street where we played "kick the can", the walk to Dixon School, my dog "Corky", my friends homes, so much and so long ago. I didn't exactly feel out of place, I just felt larger; I wanted to sit down on my front porch. I silently thanked Nelson for bringing me back here again.

And thank you Tyrone. Tyrone calls himself a "multi-tasker", works Internal Affairs Division at the police department, has a passionate hobby training dogs, three of which we met, a giant Schnauzer, a small Schnauzer and a Doberman puppy. Tyrone's passion also includes the piano and organ, involvement in his church and mostly being a husband and father. All of this and he so graciously found time to talk with me and Jim about his good friend and barber, Nelson Anderson.

Prior to working with the police dept the past 20 years, Tyrone taught Industrial Education for 12 years at Collins High School in Chicago. He and his lovely wife Donna have two children, a daughter and a son and told me Nelson loved the children.

"Every Friday, we would get a haircut and he would say, 'I enjoy when you come.' He would give the kids cookies and peppermint he got from one of his favorite restaurants, Old Country Buffet. The kids called him, 'Barber'. I believe Mr. Anderson adopted us; he came to every birthday party and all our family occasions. We always bought him Christmas presents, usually something to do with golf. I'll bet I first met Mr. Anderson 30 years ago. He knew my father who was tight with Prince, Mr. Anderson's uncle, who had a barber shop on 59th St. He and Mr. Anderson would talk about the Army; they were both very traditional men. Yes, I met Prince, long straight hair, light skinned, he moved to 79th St.

"79th St., known as the 'happening street', was lively in the 60's and 70's. It was a black middle class traditional setting. Two doors down from Mr. Anderson's barber shop was the Tiger Lounge. The older guys would get a haircut then go to the Tiger Lounge and have a drink in the early evening. Mr. Anderson watched his street go up and down with change and he enjoyed it but he didn't change. He was quiet, very alert and always concerned about everyone.

"He was traditional, a real barber in the sense that he was picky about his customers. He talked about golf, his cars and the Post Office. We talked about dogs, yes, he told me about his dog Fritz. I guess as he got older he kind of slipped a little, well sometimes the line on my hair was crooked and my moustache was a little off, but he was so accommodating. I would not have gone anywhere else.

"He was a private person with a private life and I wondered if he had been hurt by someone in this lifetime. I even thought he was kind of indigent and one time I asked him if he would come and live with us. I told him it would be an honor but he said 'No, I'm all right, but I'll think about it.' 79th St. had it all for him; I didn't know he had a barber shop on 95th St. I was flabbergasted to learn he even had money, he never let on. In fact when I think about it, I am so mad at him for not enjoying himself. I guess he was happy doing what he did. When I got promoted, he came to my graduation. And when I got the "National Organization of Black Law Enforcement Executive Award" in 1998, he was there. He sat in the last row and when they asked my people to stand, he didn't. I yelled, 'Hey, there's my friend Mr. Anderson, stand up.' We loved him!"

Tyrone Jordan has received 40 honorable mentions, four department commendations and Nelson attended them all. Both men are Chicago's finest. We said our goodbyes, hugged and Jim and I took a walk around my block, for old times.

James Richard White

"He kept his cards close to his chest." That expression said it all. He was referring to Nelson. "We were 18 years old, in a small five-man medical unit in the Army, we were best friends. I miss him. He was the only barber I ever had; in fact, he was the last one to cut my hair in July '05. I haven't had a hair cut since he died. You're right, it's over two years. I don't have that much anymore. We both would have turned 82 in July. I'm July 11, 1926 and he was July 18, 1926. "

This was James "Richard" White speaking fondly of his friend Junior. "Mostly I'd call him Junior, sometimes Nelson, he liked the name Nelson. When I saw him at the nursing home, I was shocked. There he was lying there, confused, dementia and probably didn't know he had his leg amputated.

"I never knew he was diabetic, if I had I certainly would have kept after him about his eating. He liked to explore different restaurants. I don't know if he knew me or not, there was no response, no eye contact, he just laid there in bed, so small. I tried to make conversation and reminded him of the time he picked up the check the last time we had dinner. He became more generous in his older age and he said 'Yeah', that was all. It was kind of funny the way he said it, I had to laugh. I catch myself sometimes sounding just like him and I laugh, and think of him."

This was a phone conversation I had with Mr. White. He told me he had pictures of he and Nelson and we made plans to meet for breakfast.

Yolk Restaurant, 1120 S. Michigan Ave., Chicago, June 16, 2008. I invited Michael Anderson to meet Mr. White and myself for breakfast. It was a cool sunny day, a beautiful morning to reminisce. It was good to see Michael again; we hugged, he looked good, more relaxed and more confident of himself. I was happy for him. We sat in the restaurant looking out the window waiting for Mr. White. Michael asked me if I'd ever met him before and I said, "No, but I'll know him when I see him." I saw him coming down the street, a happy looking man with a gingerly step. My first thought was, "He looks a little like Nelson with a moustache and happy-go-lucky."

And he was. We introduced ourselves to Mr. White. He told Michael he had known his father Charles and mentioned how much Michael resembled Nelson in facial features. Michael said he had heard that before and he seemed pleased.

Mr. White, another gentle mannered friend of Nelson's, small in stature, big, I mean really big in education and knowledge. He seemed to welcome the opportunity to share with us his long friendship with Nelson. Michael and I sat listening in awe of his accomplishments. As he had told me before, he and Nelson were in the Army together. Nelson was right, he had told me once that Mr. White was from Burlington, Iowa and Nelson had lived in Des Moines, Iowa.

After the service they both attended the University of Iowa. Richard (I asked him if I could call him that, silly) graduated in 1950 with a degree in Psychology and Nelson completed only one year. Nelson decided he didn't want to be a dentist after all and chose to attend Barber College. They both reunited back in Chicago after Richard completed college. The two were best friends. Richard had copied some pictures for me of he and Nelson and you'll never guess! Jerry Wolfe also! He smiled proudly when he showed us the pictures. They were pals, handsome and happy looking, and Jerry, Wow! Beautiful, actually, she hasn't changed.

Richard talked about a college degree and no job. "It was the times." He worked as a stock boy in an auto shop, someone told him not to tell anyone he had a degree or they'd think he wasn't going to stay. He made 82 cents an hour. He was a bus boy at the Hillman Cafeteria, he washed dishes in the Garland Building and he took the Civil Service Exam. His new job was as a case worker for the Welfare Department making $200 a month. He became a supervisor and in 1958 was awarded a scholarship from the State of Illinois (one of the first to be awarded by the State of Illinois) to the University of Michigan in Ann Arbor to do graduate work. Richard graduated with a Master's Degree in Social Work.

An inspiration for Richard was his professor and advisor, Wilbur J. Cohen, a leader in public welfare. In 1935 Professor Cohen helped to write the Social Security Act with President Franklin D. Roosevelt. Richard gained a G.S. (general schedule) 13 working with the Health, Education and Welfare Department in New York and Washington, D.C. Again he worked with Professor Cohen, who had left the University of Michigan in 1961 and became the assistant secretary of HEW. Richard tells a story of sitting in Wilbur Cohen's office and President John F. Kennedy phoned to speak with the secretary. Richard remained seated in the office, proud to listen in on their conversation.

In 1966, Richard was selected to be a resource person on a panel of civil rights leaders. This was for the White House Conference on Civil Rights. It was indeed an honor. He attended the NAACP banquet where he met Martin Luther King, a greater honor. Secretary Cohen proudly introduced Richard to everyone as a former student. Throughout the years he either saw or kept in touch with Nelson. He remembers saying, "Nelson, what's little old me doing here?" I'd say you're doing a good job, very impressive. In 1968 back in Chicago, Richard became the Deputy Director of WIND, a work incentive program, which led him to become Chief of Head Start, a division of Child Care Services. But he went on to accomplish more. In 1970 long term training was offered, a University of California scholarship for graduate school with a Master's Degree in Public Administration, always keeping Nelson updated of his success. Richard retired in September of 1986 from the United States Office of Human Development Services. I'll say it again, very impressive.

Nelson and Richards's friendship held together like glue all those years, the same as with his other friends. Richard talked of how he and Nelson would exchange information and advice about finances. I asked him if he knew Nelson bought the barber shop on 95th St. after Charles died. He said, "No, no I didn't." He was right, Nelson sure did keep his cards close to his chest.

Richard White, lady friends, Nelson Anderson

Richard talked of Nelson's love of travel. He said if Nelson knew you had family in other areas, he'd stop to see them when he traveled. He spoke of how Nelson loved driving his Volkswagen across country and how crazy he was about golfing. We used to play golf at the Jackson Park course that seemed to be our favorite. We'd drive around in his 1955 Ford Fairlane; he loved cars. I used to say to him, "Nelson you're a free agent, you don't have anything to worry about, no house, no furniture, no wife, no

Nelson and Richard

children, you've got the barber shop, what are you going to do with all your money? I'd kid him about the light in the bathroom in the barber shop, it was so dim. I think it hung by an extension cord. I'd tell him to put a brighter bulb in it, he never did, you were lucky you had toilet paper." Richard said Nelson liked to go in the back of the shop and play the alto sax alone.

Geraldine Wolfe and Nelson

I felt sad, did he really live behind the shop? Richard said years ago Nelson lived with a family on Vernon Avenue. He remembered they had a daughter named Nancy, but that was years ago. Michael thought he may have rented a sleeping room near the barber shop and paid cash each week. We never found receipts; we'll never know.

Richard spoke fondly of his family, a daughter, a granddaughter, a great-grandson, 17, and a great-grand daughter who was 5 years old. I encouraged him to write his own memoirs, and I thanked him for sharing his memories with me. We hugged, naturally. I would remember him on his birthday with a prayer and a card.

On August 18, 2008, we drove to Chicago to see Ruth and Tamara on a very hot and humid afternoon. I said to Jim, "Let's stop and get some flowers for Ruth. I'll watch for a florist." We were driving on West Fullerton Ave.

when I saw a flower shop and Jim pulled over. It was a bus stop so he couldn't park and told me he'd drive around the block and come back for me. Not a problem. I stepped out of the car, turned and walked straight into two plainclothes Chicago Police Officers in bullet proof vests putting hand cuffs on a young man. I hesitated then walked around them thinking, "Oh boy, what am I doing here?" I went into the store to buy flowers, came out and looked around for Jim. I was hoping the block was not too long; here he comes walking down the street. He can't wait to tell me about the police car that pulled in front of him into an alley and about the policeman that arrested two girls. I had my own story, now there were three in handcuffs. This has nothing to do with my story, but it made Jim and I laugh…Bonnie and Clyde again!

Ruth Williams Tamara Tate

"Remember when I said I wanted to buy my Mother a mansion? Well I did! I prayed about it and told my real estate lady to show me 23 houses. I dreamt I should see 5. When I saw this one I knew…I'm settled with one purpose, to make Mama happy. I gave a testimony in church of how thankful I am of my Mother."

And there sat Mama, just like a queen on a throne, so full of pride and smiling at Jim and me as we walked through the door of her mansion.

We had come to visit with Ruth Williams and Tamara Tate in their newly purchased home on the northwest side of Chicago. Ruth is Nelson's half sister and Tamara is her daughter. They are both lovely ladies, petite in stature; I don't think Ruth even came up to my shoulder when she stood up using her cane to steady herself. Tamara stayed close by in a protective manner. We had met once before at the funeral home two years ago; we laughed and hugged and all started talking at the same time. Tamara, very excitedly showed us around the house. I admit I became a little teary, how wonderful this inheritance was for the family. I truly believe Nelson would have wanted this. Like all of us he probably thought he had all kinds of time to put things together. And now…Tamara had her space on the second floor, her son Michael had the basement all fixed up and Ruth was on the first floor close to all if needed. Tamara had fitted Ruth's bathtub with a power lift and all the bells and whistles for her safety.

We met the family cat "Mister." Tamara served us cake and iced tea, wonderful on such a hot day. We began looking at pictures from Ruth's past, ones of her mother, Myrtle Mayberry Bandy, some snapshots of Nelson and one of Martha Brown. I said "the" Martha Brown? Ruth laughed and said, "My mother Myrtle knew Nelson's mother Ruth. I was named after his mother. Yes, Aunt Martha was famous; she introduced my mother to "NJ" (Nelson Sr.). They never married. The Anderson's told him "all the money would be cut off." My stepfather was Will Bandy who married my mother before I was born. NJ was not allowed to see me as we were from the north side of Nashville and he was from the south. They were an affluent black family."

Ruth spoke in a quiet voice, never taking her eyes off me and seemed glad to be able to share her memories with me. She is so sweet. Ruth was born and raised in Nashville, Tennessee in

1924. She remembers visiting with Nelson's family, Aunt Martha and Grandmother Lutie with her mother as a young girl but never knowing that "those boys" were her brothers. "Others knew it but I never did. Ruth's family (Nelson's mother), the McKissack's, built the school I went to as a young girl".

Ruth continues saying in the 40's, she was 17 and remembers not being able to go to the movie theater on the weekends because of the soldiers coming into town from the Army bases. One base was for blacks only and the other was for whites. "I remember they would line the streets, blacks on one side and whites on the other, no, no trouble, it's just that young ladies couldn't go out by themselves. Do you know the theater had a door for blacks and one for whites?"

"After Nelson's mother Ruth died, NJ married Ella, Nelson would tell me in later years he thought "she was nosy." I remember when NJ died I went to my grandmother Lutie's house; he was laid out there. I remember putting my hand over his heart. Grandmother Lutie would tell me, "A lot of things happened that she had no control over." I was just glad to be approved. I saw pictures at the funeral; the brothers knew they had a sister."

"My mother was afraid for me to stay in Nashville, so we moved to Chicago when I was 17. We stayed with my mother's sister who was sick, very caring people but grandfather Mayberry had a curfew of 9P.M. and that was hard for me. I remember him coming to unlock the door for me in his red flannels. Those hours were too restricting for me." I married in 1949 and worked at an electronics store on Van Buren St."

"My mother always kept in touch with Martha Brown who was a librarian at Tennessee State University. I believe it was Aunt Elizabeth and Aunt Jennie Lee who raised the boys in Iowa. Later Aunt Elizabeth left the house to Joseph. (Jim and I remembered that in later years Nelson had the house razed after many renters were delinquent on their rent. Nelson still continued to pay the taxes on the empty property.)

Ruth continued, "I first met Nelson when he came home on leave from the service. He came to my mother's house for a party; his uncle Ed told my mother she had a "son". I met Charles later and Nelson told me "my brother Joseph, he's a loner." I was glad to meet more folks; Nelson and I danced together. He had been in the Philippines and I remember him telling me that the Anderson's had some people in Manila, a family resort."

"Over the years we would talk, he'd call me at night." I'd say, "I'll bet you're cleaning your golf clubs"; he'd laugh, he loved golf. He always wanted to know about my life, my love life too. Did you know we both had double toes…the first and second ones? We would go out to eat. He bought me things, the most beautiful bracelet one time and he'd send me the prettiest cards. Every year for Christmas he sent a fruitcake and it was good. Sometimes he'd send me money. Everyone knew he had money; his brother Charles called him the "money man". I believe he had a Will, a lot not turned up yet. We were supposed to go out for my birthday on October 19, 2005 and he never called, but that had happened before, a lot of times he didn't come.

He didn't like to get too involved; he kept secret."

"I'm lost, I feel if I could just talk to him. I had no idea this was coming." I knew she meant it. Ruth also has two sons, Harrison and Emanuel. Harrison lives in Milwaukee, Wisconsin; he has six children and Emanuel in Chicago with one child. Tamara has Michael and Emmitt. Ruth is so proud of her family.

The more I sat looking at Ruth the more I thought how much she resembled Nelson. That was nice…the smile, that sweet, sweet smile.

"I can tell you what I think of him. He's the kind of man I would have liked to have married; priorities in order, he was a caretaker, so humble." This was lovingly shared by Tamara remembering her high school graduation. "He surprised me, I was so upset, my best friend was financially comfortable and her father gave her $100. I told my Dad that I thought I should get money too, and I was crying. Uncle Nelson gave me $50. I was so excited."

Tamara Tate and Ruth Williams

I felt that Tamara was also pleased that Nelson had saved the "thank you" card that she had sent him after all these years. Tamara, he saved it all, literally. Jim and I thanked them both for their hospitality, hugged and wished them well in their new home, er.... mansion.

Melvin Bryant

"Andy was a catalyst, a central figure, he knew a little about everybody. He would walk up and down 79th St. saying "Hi" to everyone. He was a stand up person, a distinguished gentleman." These words were genuinely spoken by Melvin Bryant, a long time friend and co-worker of Nelson's.

Jim and I first met Melvin at the nursing home when he was visiting Nelson, one of his many visits, another good friend who cared. He and Jim had both been Marines, they would chat about the service and Nelson would listen with a smile on his face. Melvin went on to say how he and

Nelson worked at the Post Office together. "Everyone knew when Andy was on the floor. A postal Timekeeper lets you know if you have overs or shorts, checks your times. He was well respected.

"Andy liked to eat, if you were in the barber shop and it was lunchtime he liked to take people to lunch, he always wanted to go out to eat. He liked different restaurants; no one knew he was a diabetic. He didn't talk much about himself. I know he liked to eat steak and I remember he always smoked a cigar, the ones in the little plastic holders." (That was news to me. I hadn't heard that before but I'd seen cigars in the shop.)

Melvin continued to say "Andy cut my hair when I had it, now I just shave my head. By Saturday I have gray stubble, I shave it and on Sunday for church, I'm good to go.

"I met a lot of good folks in the barber shop. We were always laughing and sharing stories, you know stories. Sometimes Andy would go to the hospital if someone was sick and needed a haircut; I'd seen him do that.

"He liked golf, he sure liked to play golf, no I didn't play. We would talk a lot about cars, Andy took good care of his cars, he liked to drive a lot. Everyone always wanted to buy his cars because he took good care of things."

Melvin and I reflected on Nelson's car trip to Dyer and the sadness of it all and how thankful we were of the outcome.

I asked Melvin to tell me a little about himself. He has been married for 49 years, four children and four grandchildren. Melvin will be 70 in December. (You would never know it to look at him, in fact none of Nelson's friends look their ages. All his friends are so active.) Melvin grew up in the Morgan Park area of Chicago. "I came through the foster system."

He and his brothers and sister were raised by a foster Mom. "She was basic, brute force, picked up whatever was close, very country. Alfreda Jones, she meant well, we really learned from her. She taught us manners, how to speak well, sex education, gardening, weeding and painting when I was about 8 or 9 years old. Then the State took us when I was about 15 and moved us to 70th and St. Lawrence with another foster family. They had two boys. The five of us were known as the "Jones boys"…trouble… I had a paper route. I had to go pick up my papers since no one wanted to cross the line." (Chicago in the 50's, I remembered it well, I was only 10 blocks south. It was Black and White.) "One time my foster Mom took me to Roseland Hospital. I had accidently been shot in the leg and they wouldn't wait on us; told us to go back home." Melvin and I reminisced about those times he remembered so well. He also remembered riding the streetcar for 15 cents and he told me about delivering whiskey orders to customers on his bike at the age of 17. "It was different times then, no big thing."

Melvin attended Parker High School and at 18 he joined the Marines. Life went on. Melvin retired from the Post Office in 1992 after 34 years. "I've always had two jobs; this is my 49th year as a painter, Bryant's Decorating Service. I like antiques, I've been looking for an antique barber chair, they are comfortable." I'd say Melvin Bryant is a pretty stand up guy too…Semper Fidelis".

Melvin Williams

"I really miss Andy, we had a lot of fun and he had a good sense of humor. I had known him at least 40 or 50 years. We worked at the Post Office together. I was a supervisor and Andy was a Timekeeper. He was very efficient, never knew him to make any mistakes. As close as we were, we'd talk every day, long hours; he never mentioned to me that he was a barber. When I found out about the shop on 79th St., I started to go to him for haircuts."

Melvin and I talked on the phone. I called him to talk about his friend Nelson. Melvin was one of many friends we had met while visiting Nelson at the hospital. He continued to tell me how he and Nelson played golf with the postal league. "We played all over, Lincoln Oaks, University Park, Pipe O Peace and Longwood. In fact, I think that was where Andy was heading when he got sick, to play 9 holes at Longwood in Crete. He always kept his clubs in the trunk of his car, always ready. I remember once he told me he had been a golf caddie when he was a teenager. He was sports minded but he sure loved golf." Melvin and I both laughed saying "a good game of golf was a good walk." Melvin continued, "I don't remember him talking about anything personal, he was private. I know he lived behind the barber shop. I only found out he was a diabetic when he was in the hospital. He was religious about eating. He liked to eat at Hard Times on 79th St. and liked soul food."

Melvin is a Korean War veteran and worked for the Chicago School System for 15 years. He has a Master's

Degree in Public Administration. He retired from the Post Office in 1989 after 39 years of service and lives with his lovely wife on the South Side of Chicago. Melvin tells me besides golfing he likes to bowl and play billiards. He was talking to me from the Skyway Bowl on 99th and Torrence Ave. Ironically, this was November 4, 2008, exactly three years ago that Jim and I had become guardians for Nelson. This day was also the Presidential Election Day. Melvin said he had just voted and was "keeping his fingers crossed."

Melvin, you can uncross your fingers…history was made!

Neal Gillie

"He was a private person, not very outgoing, but he was a part of a great many people's lives. I knew Andy in excess of 40 years. He was an avid golfer. I first met him on the golf course, Deer Creek in the south suburbs. Of course that was when gas was 34 cents a gallon. I'd see him on a regular basis, either at the barber shop or on the golf course. We liked to play Pipe O'Peace course on Halsted St." Fond memories expressed by Neal Gillie.

Jim and I first met Neal when he visited Nelson at the Nursing Home and then we spoke again at the funeral. Again I praised the loyalty of Nelson's friends.

Neal remembered Nelson telling him of the barber shop that Nelson's Uncle Prince had on 55th St. between Michigan and Calumet Ave. He said it was in a hotel…more history. "Mavis cut my hair first until she left then Andy the last 20 years. We'd talk about current events and sports mostly. The barber shop was very clean and I don't think he changed anything over the years. He liked to go to Nashville to the Ted Rhodes Tournament. Oh, he always went by himself, he'd get in his car and go, sometimes for weeks." (Ted Rhodes (1913- 1969) was recognized as the first African American professional golfer from Nashville, Tennessee. Ted introduced Joe Louis, the professional boxer, to the game of golf and became his teacher, even traveled with him to later become his valet.)

Neal was born and raised in Chicago, 60th and Wabash; at present he is semi-retired working as a real estate appraiser. For 30 years he owned and operated the "19th Hole" lounge at 9705 S. Halsted St. from January 1963 until November 1991.

Neal, proudly mentioned being the father of two children and grandfather of two. He still resides on the South Side of Chicago.

Johnny Johnson

"We're not all cut from the same cloth, sure he was closed, maybe an introvert, but he was so dedicated and friendly, he'd go out of his way for you." John worked with Nelson at the Post Office. He was a supervisor when Nelson was the Timekeeper; he knew him since the late 50's. Nelson also was John's barber in later years. I asked him what they talked about and he said "the barber shop, it was a gossip den, from females to politics, we all talked about everything... current events...we kept up. I used to kid Andy about the old

Volkswagen. When you going to get a new ride? We talked about music. I remember he told me about his cousin, Doc Cheatham who played Dixieland. I recorded some tapes for him to play on his 8-track as he loved music."

I told John I grew up in Chatham and we talked about 79th St. He remembered going to the Rhodes Theater before they tore it down and the Chatham Bowl. We laughed. John said he retired from the Post Office in 1989. "I'm not a young gay blade anymore, but I don't sit on my haunches either."

Today is Veterans Day, November 11; John served in the Navy in 1945-1946 and in the Army in Korea 1951-1953. Thank you for your service, John. I reminded him of our conversation two weeks after Nelson's funeral, how inspirational he was for me. I never forgot his words.

"Thank you for doing right by my friend Andy."

Robert Ward

"I met Junior in 1946 when we both worked at the Airmail Post Office at Midway Airport. Yes, we all called him 'Junior'. He worked there until it closed, then he went to the main office when I transferred to the La Salle St. Station. When Junior became a barber, he cut my hair. Yes, I remember his Uncle Prince, he was a braggadocio, a big talker, bragged about everything, the opposite of Junior."

I remembered meeting Robert at the hospital and at the nursing home, another caring friend.

Robert remembered that Prince had a barber shop on 63rd St., and then moved to 55th St. where he and Nelson would go to lunch to a restaurant called "Kiah" after he got his hair cut. Then the shop moved to 79th St. where Nelson cut his hair and they still lunched together. Robert went on to say that his friend loved golfing and that he made many trips to Biloxi in his Volkswagen to play golf.

"He knew my family and we saw him often. He knew all my kids. I'm widowed now…my wife died…I have six children and seven grandchildren and 'a few' great-grandchildren. I remember Junior didn't always live behind the barber shop. He lived with a family on 85th and Prairie; yes, they had a daughter named Nancy." (Again, memories of Nancy. Nancy, if you read this, please call me.)

Robert worked two jobs for a while, the post office, went to college and then became a teacher in 1957 working in the Englewood School System as a teacher, a counselor and eventually Assistant Principal. By that time in 1964 he had resigned from the Post Office and in 1972 he worked for the Board Of Education as Director of Insurance and Employee Benefits. He retired in 1985.

Francis Lee

I had a lovely conversation with Francis Lee, who proudly told me she was 80 years old. I had heard her name in connection with Nelson's as maybe being a girlfriend. Sure enough, they dated for about 15 months. I had written her a note and she called me back, speaking in almost a whisper, gladly sharing her memories of Nelson with me.

She recalled, "I had been divorced with two young children and a friend introduced me to Nelson; that was in 1968. Nelson really liked the children and we would take them to eat at Fred and Jack's Restaurant on 75th and the Dan Ryan. Nelson drove a Volkswagen and he also had a Saab. He would tell my daughter that he would donate it to her when she got older but that didn't happen.

"Nelson liked to eat and he liked to go to Hockey games. We would talk but nothing serious. He didn't talk much about his family. I know he had an uncle in Savannah, Georgia and I had met his uncle Prince who owned the barber shop on 79th St. He was very fond of him. Sometimes we went to Joliet to visit some friends of Nelson's, a doctor and his wife; they may have been related.

"Nelson had gone to Wilson Junior College for one year; he had wanted to be a dentist. I don't know why he dropped out. I guess he changed his mind. I remember he lived with a family on 85th St., he rented a room in a ladies home and he was very conservative. He was also secretive, but wasn't he nice. You liked him too, didn't you?

"In later years I would take my grandson to the barber shop for a haircut and I remember one time he came to my church, the Chicago Temple downtown with a lady friend. I don't know what happened but we just drifted away."

Francis, a teacher, retired from the Chicago Public School System in 1989 after over 39 years. Francis now lives with her daughter on the South Side of

Chicago. She has two grandchildren and is a lovely lady.

During our conversation Francis asked me where Nelson was buried and I told her about Greenwood Cemetery in Nashville, Tennessee and the family plot. She seemed pleased to know Nelson was with his parents and grandmother, and then (honestly) she asked me if Nelson had a tombstone… could be a lead in to a fine ending for my story.

The heirs to Nelson's estate are:

Ruth Williams
Michael Anderson
Sharon Osborn
Joseph Anderson

If you're ever in Nashville, take a ride by Greenwood Cemetery...pay your respects, say a prayer or maybe leave a flower in the vase...

If you walk down 79th St. in Chicago, be proud, a lot of good folks, a lot of good memories travel with you of a rich and celebrated history...

Friends and family we have had the pleasure of knowing:

Michael Anderson
Irma Adams
William Blair
Sharon Osborn
Bernice Gibson
Russell London
Moses Jones
Milton Williams
Richard Douglas
Clifton Martin
John Turner
Huey Scott
Reverend Nicholas Taylor
Joyce Franklin
Louise Williams (Wezee)
Sgt. Tyrone Jordan
James "Richard" White
Bob Seymour
Ruth Williams
Tamara Tate
J.C. McCoy
Mavis Sims

Ted Lawson
Melvin Williams
Thomas Banks
Geraldine Wolfe
Vesta Cole
Neal Gillie
Robert Ward
John Johnson
Frances Lee
Ted Lawson
Muriel Glenn

Ruth William's Family Portrait on her 85th Birthday

Joan Bodefeld, born and raised on the South Side of Chicago, attended Dixon Grade School, Hirsch High School and graduated in 1960 from South Chicago Community Hospital School of Nursing. Mother of three, daughter Mary Davis, sons Steve and Dave Ainley. Proud grandmother of nine, Michael and Ben Davis, Steven, Michelle, Dylan, Hannah, Samantha Ainley, Danny and Diane Ainley. Retired from St. Margaret Mercy Health Care Center in Dyer, Indiana after many years of joyful service. Enjoys reading, gardening, crocheting, golfing, baking, traveling, crossword puzzles and activities with the grandkids. Joan also spends time crocheting 'prayer shawls' with her long time good friend and golf buddy, Evelyn Musial. These shawls are donated to the St. Stephen Ministry in Tinley Park, Illinois for distribution to those in need.

James Bodefeld, born and raised in Whiting, Indiana, attended Sacred Heart Grade School, Clark High School, Indiana University and served in the United States Marine Corp. Father of Jim who resides with his wife Pam, and their daughters, Mellisa and Isobel in Katy, Texas, son Brent who lives in Chicago, Illinois. Jim is retired and enjoys traveling, golfing, reading and time spent with family and grandchildren.

Joan and Jim live in Dyer, Indiana, are active in the Peace Lutheran Church, Schererville, Indiana (Dan Dierks, Pastor) and continue to volunteer for VAS. Both enjoy long walks in Plum Creek Forest Preserve with their Airedale “Duffy”.

WHO WAS THIS LITTLE BIG MAN?

This is a story of a man whose life was full of meaning and wealth (not monetarily but in friendships). Nelson Anderson was the kind of man you could not help but love. He was unassuming, kindhearted, generous, and quiet, a man who had a long line of friends. Here was a man who took the life he had been given and silently, without pomp and ceremony, turned it to gold.

Nelson was a simple yet complex man who chose to live in a way where he could help others. It was this simple life that drew others to him. He was a barber who cut hair for a pittance not because he had to but because that's how he was.

Nelson Anderson left this world on February 22, 2006. He made that last journey in the way he had lived… quietly and unassumingly. He knew St. Peter had the door open waiting for him to arrive. There is no doubt that when he did arrive St. Peter would have asked:

"How are you Nelson?"

Then with his captivating smile and soft spoken voice, Nelson would have replied.

"Well, you know."

'It is not the metal of a man's mind but the love in his heart for which he should be remembered.'

Michael Blackett
Publisher and Author

Printed in the United States
214357BV00004B/4/P

9 781607 434382